ADVANCED PRAISE FOR
THE FOURTH WAY: THE INSPIRING FUTURE FOR EDUCATIONAL CHANGE

By **Andy Hargreaves and Dennis Shirley**

"Andy Hargreaves and Dennis Shirley provide a wonderful and international perspective on the educational movements we have passed through. They describe what was and was not effective in each, and a good picture of the way forward. The new era— the Fourth Way—holds more than just promise. Elements of this approach are underway in different parts of the world at this very moment and the authors shine light on each as they encourage the reader to tap into the very best practices to assure the next wave truly leaves no child, family, or community behind!"

—Alan Blankstein
President
Hope Foundation

"The authors propose a new vision for transforming public education for the 21st century. They argue that school systems must move away from a culture of high-stakes testing, encourage innovation and creativity, and engage parents and communities in educational change. Their ideas are timely ~~and~~ ~~~~ *educational leaders today."*

D1111871

American Association ~~of School Administrators~~

"Perplexed and demoralized by policies that diminish and routinize their work, many educators fear that public schooling has reached a dead end. In this informed and inspiring book, Hargreaves and Shirley point to a new and promising path for progress. The Fourth Way, as they explain, is not only open to educators, but must be forged by them, with shared purpose, foresight, and common sense."

—Susan Moore Johnson
Pforzheimer Professor of Teaching and Learning
Harvard University

"In this timely and inspirational book, Andy Hargreaves and Dennis Shirley challenge our current thinking about educational change. Their argument for interdependence, empowerment, collective courage, and professionalism will resonate with all who have wrestled with these issues. It will leave a lasting impression. Read it!"

—Steve Munby
Chief Executive
National College for School Leadership, England

"This is a great book! Andy Hargreaves and Dennis Shirley have an incredible ability to describe important issues in incisive and compelling ways."

—Dennis Sparks
Emeritus Executive Director
National Staff Development Council

The

FOURTH
WAY

ANDY HARGREAVES • DENNIS SHIRLEY

The

FOURTH
WAY
The Inspiring Future
for Educational Change

A JOINT
PUBLICATION

CORWIN
A SAGE Company

ONTARIO
PRINCIPALS'
COUNCIL
Exemplary Leadership
in Public Education

10/23/09
Lan
$25.95

For information:

Corwin
A SAGE Company
2455 Teller Road
Thousand Oaks, California 91320
(800) 233-9936
Fax: (800) 417-2466
www.corwinpress.com

SAGE India Pvt. Ltd.
B 1/I 1 Mohan Cooperative
Industrial Area
Mathura Road, New Delhi 110 044
India

SAGE Ltd.
1 Oliver's Yard
55 City Road
London EC1Y 1SP
United Kingdom

SAGE Asia-Pacific Pte. Ltd.
33 Pekin Street #02-01
Far East Square
Singapore 048763

Printed in the United States of America.

Library of Congress Cataloging-in-Publication Data

Hargreaves, Andy.
The fourth way: The inspiring future for educational change/Andy Hargreaves, Dennis Shirley.
p. cm.
"A Joint publication with the Ontario Principal's Council and the National Staff Development Council."
Includes bibliographical references and index.
ISBN 978-1-4129-7637-4 (pbk. : alk. paper)
1. Educational change--Cross-cultural studies. 2. Comparative education. 3. Education and state—Cross-cultural studies. 4. Motivation in education—Cross-cultural studies. I. Shirley, Dennis, 1955- II. Title.

LB43.H37 2009
370.9—dc22   2009011206

This book is printed on acid-free paper.

09   10   11   12   13   10   9   8   7   6   5   4   3   2   1

Acquisitions Editor:	Arnis Burvikovs
Associate Editor:	Desirée A. Bartlett
Production Editor:	Eric Garner
Copy Editor:	Alison Hope
Typesetter:	C&M Digitals (P) Ltd.
Proofreader:	Theresa Kay
Indexer:	Molly Hall
Cover Designer:	Scott Van Atta with Jay Lim

CONTENTS

PREFACE

▪▪

This book comes at the end of a decade of great growth and apparent prosperity. Middle-class America, like the middle classes in many other developed economies, became a culture of shopping, spending, and speculation. Even moderate middle-class earners turned into property owners and speculators, boosting consumer spending and incurring increasing debt with the confidence that ever-rising property values would cover their credit. Meanwhile, those on the lower rungs of the middle and working classes saw their real incomes fall and borrowed more and more money on increasingly risky terms to make ends meet and avoid getting left behind.

But the boom is over. Housing prices are in free fall and the credit crunch is on. Big-time investors played and lost with ordinary people's money, our governments stepped in to bail them out, and we will be paying the price and repaying the debt for years to come. So who needs another book on educational change at this crucial moment in our shared economic destiny? Isn't it time to just hold things right where they are, to put education and schools on the back burner, and attend to bigger priorities instead?

There are those who have said that the greatest financial crisis since the Great Depression should cause us to freeze all public spending at current levels and that boosting public education is a luxury we can no longer afford. They have argued that now is the time to cut back, just as we did in the 1980s. Yet, in *When Markets Collide*, economic and investment guru Mohammed El-Erian reminds us that it is exactly when we are in a slump and falling behind international competitors, such as the emerging economies, of China, India, and parts of the Middle East, that we most need to invest in the training and skills that will shape our future.[1]

Then there are those who produce fear-mongering books and videos that depict how much harder and longer the children and young adults of Asian economies work in order to get ahead. We learn about young people who take extra calculus for pleasure, go to cramming schools on the weekends, and study musical instruments with relentless rigor. Like many American reformers in the 1990s argued after visits to Japan, these commentators propose harder work, longer hours, and increased diligence as the savior of our overindulged adolescents.[2] Of course, more emphasis on hard work compared to making easy money or wanting instant fame is certainly a good thing. But hard work alone is not enough. Indeed, the New Puritans of school reform who see increased effort as the answer overlook the problematic aspects of some of the countries with top test scores. Many of these competitors are rarely or barely democracies. Civic engagement is often sacrificed for personal advancement, humanitarianism is sometimes a casualty of increased entrepreneurialism, and social studies and the humanities can mean content memorization and drill rather than critical and independent thinking.

Then there are those who see in Chinese and Indian spaceships the same economic and educational threats that U.S. politicians saw in the Soviet Union's launch of Sputnik in 1957. And their answers are equally askew—more science, mathematics, and technology; less art, music, physical education, history, and literature.[3] These pundits ignore how the world's most educationally and economically successful democracies do not succeed by science and mathematics alone, or by just throwing more content at young people as if they were force-fed geese. Instead, these nations prosper through a broad and challenging curriculum that teaches people what to do with knowledge, how to apply it and move it around among others, and how to come up with new knowledge when change requires it. These prosperous democracies are successful knowledge societies.

Finally, there are those who believe that people in business have the answer to educational change and that they know best where to go next. They want more data and performance targets. They advise more competition among schools, along with performance-based pay for teachers—proposing that young and hungry teachers would gladly choose a more front-loaded salary they could invest in a stock-market pension of defined contributions rather than gradually accumulating rewards that lead to defined benefits.[4] After the catastrophic collapse of the free market and the stock market, along with the loss of many people's defined-contribution pensions, these undiscriminating business admirers must now feel a bit embarrassed, at best.

At a time of global economic meltdown, increasing dependence on oil, and accelerating climate change, we need bold new solutions, not stale old slogans. Cutbacks do not equip us to be competitive in the future. The unregulated markets that got us into our current financial mess and pushed market-driven solutions into the public sector are not going to get us out of it. Educational standardization has dumbed down our curriculum and burdened our schools with bigger government and overbearing bureaucracy, and has not enabled us to adapt flexibly to the future. These Old Ways of educational change in the 20th century are ill suited to the fast, flexible, and vulnerable New World of the 21st century.

It is time, now more than ever, for a New Way of educational change that is suited to the dramatically new problems and challenges we are encountering. This New Way should build on the best of what we have learned from the Old Ways of the past without retreating to or reinventing the worst of them. It should look abroad for intelligent alternatives and be especially alert to those educational and economic successes that also express and advance democratic and humanitarian values. It should attend to the advancement of the economy and the restoration of prosperity but not at the price of other educational elements that contribute to the development of personal integrity, social democracy, and the advancement of human decency.

This book sets out such a way of educational and social change: the *Fourth Way*. Caught writing part of this book in a local coffee shop, a customer at a neighboring table, perhaps bored with his date (or maybe she was bored with him), leaned over and asked what we were writing. On being told this was a book called *The Fourth Way*, he retorted, "Wow, that's really interesting." Asked why, he replied, "Because it really makes me wonder what the other three are!"

We hope you will have the same response. We identify three prior Ways of change since World War II and then describe foundational principles of a new Fourth Way of change. Among the alternatives from which we can choose as we pass today's critical turning point, it is the Fourth Way that will move us towards a more inclusive, inspiring, and sustainable future.

Our argument is a kind of journey. It begins with a first chapter that sets out the three Ways of change that have gone before:

- a First Way of state support and professional freedom, of innovation but also inconsistency;
- a Second Way of market competition and educational standardization in which professional autonomy is lost; and
- a Third Way that tries to navigate between and beyond the market and the state and balance professional autonomy with accountability.

Chapter 1 identifies the legacies each Way has left us and distinguishes what we should keep or retrieve, and what we should leave behind.

In Chapter 2, we argue that the great promise of the Third Way has not been fulfilled because three paths of distraction have diverted us from it: (1) autocratic imposition of targets and testing, (2) technocratic obsessions with data and spreadsheets, and (3) effervescent indulgence in securing quick lifts in test gains. These distractions make education short sighted and superficial, preventing deeper transformations in the quality of teaching and learning that can produce higher-order thinking skills and develop deeper virtues and values.

Chapter 3 delineates four horizons of hope—images of promising practice that give clues about the most desirable way forward. These images comprise the world's highest-performing nation on many international indicators of educational and economic success, the most turned-around school district in England, a professional network of 300 underachieving schools that improved results dramatically by promoting schools working with schools, and outstanding instances of community organizing and development that demonstrate how positive change does not always begin with government but must sometimes work aside from and even in opposition to it.

Building on these research-based examples, we set out the new direction of the Fourth Way in Chapter 4 by describing six pillars of purpose that support change, three principles of professionalism that drive it, and four catalysts of coherence that hold it together.

All the elements of the Fourth Way we point to are real. Every one of them already exists. We have seen them with our own eyes in the nations, networks, and systems we have evaluated and in the schools with which we work. We describe them fully in this book. These examples are not selective and rose-tinted celebrations of success based on second-hand sources or swift visits to districts to listen to senior leaders praise their own systems in ways that echo our own biases. We pinpoint the limitations as well as strengths of our examples and show how we can and should push beyond them. In this respect, the Fourth Way is based upon substantial first-hand assessments of high performing systems and promising practices from around the world.

A world dominated by wealth and might has diminished and almost destroyed us. But in the depths of crisis, a new spirit is emerging in which service and sacrifice in a commonwealth of hope can elevate us to a higher purpose and a humane exercise of our powers. The song lines from Leonard Cohen that we have selected to open this volume remind us that historical change is real, not illusory. Greed and a culture of narcissism can give way to public spirit. Secrecy and surveillance can give way to transparency and democracy. There is no finer place to pursue this quest than through the education of the young—the generations of our future. This is the moment that has summoned our effort to chart a better course in social and educational change—a Fourth Way of innovation, inspiration, and sustainability.

ACKNOWLEDGMENTS

——— ∷ ———

No book like this is ever the product of solitary scholarship. We could never have undertaken or completed this manuscript without the immeasurable patience, candid feedback, and humbling humor of our wives, Pauline and Shelley. They endured mountains of clutter strewn across the furniture and stuffed inside our heads as we worked through endless drafts of this book. Their understanding and encouragement have meant the world to us both in personal and professional terms as they have reflected with us on their own realities in teaching and school administration, and on how these relate to the arguments of our book.

We would like to thank Alan Boyle, J.-C. Couture, Linda Darling-Hammond, Dean Fink, Michael Fullan, Atul Gawande, Anthony Giddens, Alma Harris, Jenny Lewis, Steve Munby, Edvin Østergaard, Beatriz Pont, Vivianne Robinson, Pasi Sahlberg, Michael Schratz, Dennis Sparks, Marla Ucelli, Duncan Waite, and the doctoral students in our International Educational Change Study Group at Boston College for their close readings of the texts and their helpful comments.

The extensive research on which this book is based also comes out of stimulating and productive collaborations with valued colleagues and friends over many years. Ivor Goodson, Dean Fink, Michael Baker, Martha Foote, Corrie Giles, Shawn Moore, and Sonia James-Wilson made exceptional contributions to the Spencer Foundation–funded *Change Over Time* research in the United States and Canada on which much of our analysis of the first three Ways of change rests.[5]

Michael Evans, Corrie Stone-Johnson, and Deanna Riseman have exemplified the remarkable quality and character of graduate students with whom we are fortunate to work. In collaborating with us on evaluating the *Raising Achievement, Transforming Learning (RATL)* network in England, they offered not only indispensable support but also intellectual collegiality, personal camaraderie, and the shared commitment to social justice that sustains all of us at Boston College. *RATL* leaders in England—David Crossley and Graham Corbyn—provided exemplary support and assistance through all phases of the research activity, and we have learned much of enduring value from them.[6]

One of us was honored to be invited by the Organisation for Economic Co-operation and Development to work with a small team to investigate and report on the relationship between leadership and school improvement in Finland—the world's leading nation on many international indicators of educational and economic performance. Beatrice Pont and Gábor Halász—the other members of this team—worked with tireless effort and exercised incisive judgment from before dawn and beyond dusk every day to make critical sense of the extensive data we were collecting.[7]

In one or two places, we draw on an ongoing project funded by England's National College for School Leadership and the Specialist Schools and Academies Trust on organizations that perform beyond expectations in education, health, business, and sport. Alma Harris is codirecting this cross-national project involving research teams from the United States and England with one of us. Alan Boyle has worked most directly on the two examples discussed here of a high-performing local authority and a professional sports team that uses performance data to advance improvement.

A key part of our argument is about the importance of engaging parents and communities in educational change. Wendy Puriefoy, Marion Orr, and John Rogers with the Scholars Forum of the Public Education Network in the United States have informed and inspired us through rich conversations that have made clear the necessity and the nature of community organizing.[8] President Barack Obama may have brought community organizing into the public eye, but the everyday community organizers with whom one of us has been privileged to work have lifted up the educational and social contributions and achievements of some of America's most challenged and politically neglected communities for decades.

Elizabeth MacDonald and the Boston Public School teachers in the *Mindful Teacher Project* funded by the Boston Collaborative Fellows have kept us grounded in and inspired by the everyday lives as well as the vocational commitments of classroom teachers and especially those who choose to teach in urban schools.[9] They have reminded us repeatedly why this work must be done; through their positive examples, they have motivated us to keep going.

As we have written this book and undertaken the research behind it, we have become good colleagues and good friends. We have worked through the ideas, evidence, and frustrations in our offices and homes and at a number of conference venues, but two places retain special importance for us. The staff of the Busy Bee Diner in Brookline, Massachusetts, have served us many fine breakfasts over the past two years and often endured our professorial absentmindedness in forgetting what we want to order or even how to pay the bill! The creators and maintainers of the Appalachian Trail have provided us and many others with a truly inspiring and sustainable environment where, literally as well as figuratively, we could walk through the ideas at the heart of our work. The Trail is an ecological testament to the energizing relationship between sound conservation and good conversation.

Last but not least, we could be in no finer place than the Lynch School of Education at Boston College to undertake research and teaching that can have a strategic impact on educational practice. Our colleagues and graduate students have always been more than willing to give specific feedback on our work as it has unfolded. But more than this, in all our interactions and conversations, they really help us try to live up to the mission of Boston College: to pursue disciplined inquiry through service to others and with a shared commitment to social justice. Our thanks especially go to those graduate students who selflessly helped us with our diagrams and reference searches in the final frantic weeks of completing the manuscript—Kristin Kew, Michelle Reich, Randall Lahann, Kathryn Sallis, Alex Gurn, and Karla Loya.

FURTHER ACKNOWLEDGMENTS

This book has been developed from earlier and shorter versions of various parts of our argument that can be found in the following publications on which we have drawn with kind permission of the publishers.

Hargreaves, A., & Goodson, I. (Eds.). (2006). Special themed issue on *Change Over Time. Educational Administration Quarterly, 42*(1).

Hargreaves, A., Halász, G., & Pont, B. (2008). The Finnish approach to system leadership. In Pont, B., Nusche, D., & Hopkins, D. (Eds.) *Improving school leadership, Vol. 2: Case studies on system leadership*, pp. 69–109. Paris: OECD.

Hargreaves, A., & Shirley, D. (2008). Beyond standardization: Powerful new principles for improvement. *Phi Delta Kappan, 90*(2), 135–143.

Hargreaves, A., & Shirley, D. (2008, October). The fourth way of educational change. *Educational Leadership, 66*(2), 56–61.

Hargreaves, A., & Shirley, D. (2009). The persistence of presentism. *Teachers College Record, 111*(11).

Hargreaves, A., Shirley, D., Evans, M., Johnson, C., & Riseman, D. (2007). *The long and short of school improvement: Final evaluation of the* Raising Achievement, Transforming Learning *programme of the Specialist Schools and Academies Trust*. London: Specialist Schools and Academies Trust.

MacDonald, E., & Shirley, D. (2009). *The mindful teacher*. New York: Teachers College Press.

Shirley, D. (1997). *Community organizing for urban school reform*. Austin, TX: University of Texas Press.

Shirley, D. (2006). Street-level democrats: Realizing the potential of school, university, and community coalitions. *The Educational Forum, 70*(2), 116–122.

Shirley, D., & Hargreaves, A. (2006). Data-driven to distraction. *Education Week, 26*(4), 32–33.

ABOUT THE AUTHORS

Andy Hargreaves is the Thomas More Brennan Chair in the Lynch School of Education at Boston College. Prior to coming to Boston College, he taught primary school and lectured in several English universities, including Oxford. In addition, he was cofounder and director of the International Centre for Educational Change at the Ontario Institute for Studies in Education in Toronto. He has held numerous prestigious visiting professorships in Canada, Hong Kong, Japan, Sweden, Spain, the United Kingdom, and the United States. Currently, he is the elected Visiting Professor at the Institute of Education in London. He has received the Whitworth Award for outstanding contributions to educational research in Canada and was awarded a writing residency at the Villa Serbelloni in Bellagio, Italy, by the Rockefeller Foundation.

Andy is the founder and Editor-in-Chief of the *Journal of Educational Change*. He is leading editor of the first and second *International Handbooks of Educational Change*. His books have achieved outstanding writing awards from the American Educational Research Association, the American Libraries Association, and the American Association of Colleges for Teacher Education. His books have been translated into many languages. His most recent books are *Sustainable Leadership* (with Dean Fink, 2006), and *Change Wars* (with Michael Fullan, 2008). Andy presents to and consults widely with governments, foundations, teacher unions, administrator associations, and other groups across the world. His current research is on organizations that perform above expectations in education, health, business, and sport.

Dennis Shirley is professor at the Lynch School of Education at Boston College. Dennis's educational work spans from the nitty-gritty microlevel of assisting beginning teachers in complex school environments to the macrolevel of designing and guiding large-scale research and intervention projects for school districts, states, and networks. Dennis was the first U.S. scholar to document the rise of community organizing as an educational change strategy, and his activities in this arena have led to multiple long-term collaborations and a steady stream of speaking engagements and visiting professorships in Austria, Canada, Germany, Ireland, Italy, Japan, Spain, the United Kingdom, and the United States.

Along with Andy Hargreaves, Dennis publishes frequently in *Educational Leadership*, the *Phi Delta Kappan, Teachers College Record*, and *Education Week*. The two recently conducted a study of more than 300 secondary schools in the United Kingdom affiliated with the *Raising Achievement, Transforming Learning* network of the Specialist Schools and Academies Trust. In addition, they have just completed a study of the *Alberta (Canada) Initiative for School Improvement*, a network sponsoring lateral learning within and across schools in the world's second highest–achieving jurisdiction after Finland.

A fluent speaker of German, Dennis recently has spoken at and advised the Free University of Berlin, the University of Vienna, the University of Hildesheim, and the University of Dortmund on topics ranging from community engagement in schools to the reform of teacher education. At home in Boston, Massachusetts, Dennis is in the fifth year of leading a teacher inquiry seminar along with teacher leader Elizabeth MacDonald. This seminar is described in their recently published Teachers College Press book entitled *The Mindful Teacher*.

Dennis has received numerous scholarly awards, including fellowships from the Alexander von Humboldt Foundation in Bad Godesberg, Germany, and the Rockefeller Study and Conference Center in Bellagio, Italy. He holds a doctoral degree from Harvard University.

Sail on, sail on
O mighty ship of state!
To the shores of need
Past the reefs of greed
Through the squalls of hate
Sail on, sail on, sail on.

—Leonard Cohen, "Democracy"

Source: Copyright © Sony/ATV Music Publishing.

There is no debt without memory.

—MARGARET ATWOOD,
PAYBACK (2008)

CHAPTER ONE

THE THREE WAYS
OF CHANGE

The First Way of Innovation and Inconsistency

The Second Way of Markets and Standardization

The Third Way of Performance and Partnership

We are entering an age of post-standardization in education. It may not look, smell, or feel like it, but the augurs of the new age have already arrived and are advancing with increasing speed.

- Shortly before the 2008 U.S. presidential election, the chair of the U.S. House Education and Labor Committee proclaimed that the No Child Left Behind (NCLB) Act had "become the most negative brand in America." Eighty-five percent of surveyed educators agreed the NCLB was not improving schools, and a high-profile commission—including leading superintendents, CEOs, and two former secretaries of education—complained that America's obsession with tested and standardized basics was destroying its capacity to be economically creative and competitive.[1]
- In Asia, high-performing Singapore emphasizes "Teach Less, Learn More" and mandates 10% "white space" for teachers to bring individual initiative and creativity into their teaching. Meanwhile, the burgeoning economic power of China makes school-developed curriculum a national educational priority.
- The European Union names 2009 the "Year of Innovation and Creativity" in its push to give it a greater edge in economic competitiveness.[2]

1

- Finland is the world's leader on results in the OECD Programme for International Student Assessment (PISA) tests of sophisticated, applied knowledge in mathematics, science, and literacy, as well as on international ratings of economic competitiveness. Finland avoids national standardized tests altogether and reaches high levels of achievement by attracting highly qualified teachers with supportive working conditions, strong degrees of professional trust, and an inspiring mission of inclusion and creativity.[3]
- Many parents and teachers in England object to its young children being the most tested in the world. That country's government puts an end to all standardized testing in secondary schools. Wales abolishes national testing altogether up to age 14.[4] One of the leading headteachers' associations and the largest teachers' unions announces a joint conference motion to boycott the primary school tests.
- In Canada, the legislature of the conservative province of Alberta votes to abolish the Grade 3 provincial test and Nova Scotia announces the elimination of its provincial examinations in Grades 6 and 9 because they say that they are "not worth the costs."

FINDING OUR WAY

At the end of the 20th century, a new consensus emerged in most Western democracies about the best path forward for peace, prosperity, and progress. Leaders called this new path the Third Way. Prime Minister Tony Blair of Britain and Chancellor Gerhard Schröder of Germany wrote a joint paper on this Third Way.[5] President Bill Clinton convened an international meeting at the White House to discuss it, and the director of the prestigious London School of Economics, Anthony Giddens, became its theoretical guru.[6] The idea was simple: Get past the idealization of the welfare state on the one hand and the ideology of markets on the other. Instead, develop a more pragmatic path—the Germans called it "the new middle"—that would capitalize on the strengths of the welfare state and markets while minimizing their weaknesses. Above all, support policies that would reinvigorate and expand the public sphere, with the ultimate goal of increasing civic engagement among all sectors of the population.

This promising policy direction that raised high hopes around the world is now stuck—especially in education. Based on what we can learn from the past, as well as excellent alternatives at home and abroad, this book draws on years of our own research and improvement work to show how and why the Third Way has stalled. It then sets out a better way—a Fourth Way—of educational and social change to correct the course and gather momentum for a better path ahead.

The Fourth Way has not been conjured out of thin air. Almost all ideas about change start somewhere else. They can come from other countries such as Finland, Singapore, and South Korea that have strong records of educational and economic achievement as well as social cohesion, or they can come from exceptional outliers of innovative and highly effective practice within our own districts, states, provinces, and nations. We have direct experience with many of these and draw on that experience throughout the book.

The past is *also* a foreign country.[7] We bring ideas, images, and experiences of change from there, too. The past shapes our aspirations for and orientations to change in the present and the future. Knowingly or unknowingly, school leaders often take some of what worked for them in one school into the next—even when it doesn't fit. It's therefore best to have a thoughtful and reflective relationship to past experiences—including educational experiences. This way, we can accept their existence, acknowledge their influence, and sort out which aspects should be rekindled and which left behind.

Educators and reformers have already trodden other Ways; their journeys and experiences undoubtedly affect how they approach the Way ahead. We therefore begin by describing the three preceding Ways of educational change to tease out the legacies they have bequeathed to us. In these Ways, you might see some of your own journeys and struggles and appreciate how much you already know that can equip you to move ahead. The following accounts of the first two Ways of change in particular draw on Giddens's theoretical accounts of the Third Way.[8]

THE FIRST WAY OF INNOVATION AND INCONSISTENCY

The First Way was one in which the welfare state defined the status quo. It lasted from the end of World War II to the mid-1970s. In Australia, Canada, the United Kingdom, and the United States, the social safety net of the welfare state appealed to war veterans of all ranks and their families. Having made so many sacrifices, they now wanted the opportunities and freedoms for which they had fought. Economist John Maynard Keynes and his followers presented investment in state services not just as a social good but also as a benefit for the economy because it developed the pools of talent that would fuel future prosperity. The Bretton Woods Agreements, signed in a hotel in the mountains of New Hampshire, gave this strategy an international footing.

In the United States, First Way thinking came to full fruition during Lyndon Johnson's Great Society, through federal programs such as Operation Head Start for early childhood education. In Britain, Canada, and elsewhere, the new emphasis was evident in the establishment of national health services, investments in public housing, and an expansion of comprehensive secondary education and higher education. This was a period of enormous confidence in the ability of the state to solve social problems, fueled by a booming economy and spurred by the rising Baby Boomer population.

In the latter years of this age, these structural changes of state and economy catalyzed a cultural revolution. Social movements that began with the civil rights struggle expanded into protests against the Vietnam War and in favor of women's liberation. These provided avenues for historically marginalized groups to push their freedoms and proclaim their new assertiveness in the public sphere. At the same time, the first generation of economically independent adolescents invented and indulged in the freewheeling culture of rock and roll, along with the antiestablishment humor of television shows such as *Monty Python's Flying Circus* and *Laugh-In.*

This rebellious and creative spirit of the times entered public schools, albeit unevenly, in the form of experimentation, innovation, free schooling, deschooling, and teaching in primary and elementary schools that was more child centered (Figure 1.1). Idealistic educators such as Herbert Kohl and Jonathan Kozol wrote gripping narratives condemning educational injustices and advocating radical changes.[9] Even with these challenges, teachers and other state professionals had great autonomy in the First Way.

Figure 1.1   The First Way

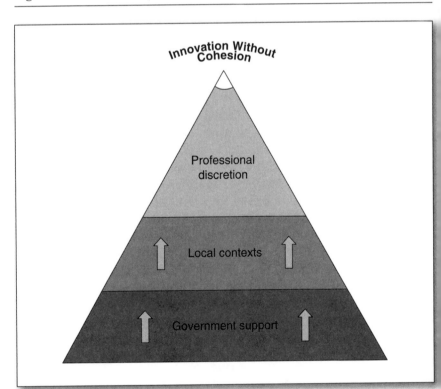

They enjoyed high levels of trust from an increasingly prosperous public, and they were left alone to get on with the job.

In a study of long-term *Change Over Time* spanning more than three decades from the 1970s to the present in eight innovative and traditional high schools in the United States and Canada, one of us found that all the schools were caught up in the zeitgeist of this First Way of social reform. Educators remembered this period as having great optimism and innovation. A high tide of liberalism led to generous outlays that reduced poverty and provided substantial government resources for schools serving the children of the most disadvantaged populations. One teacher described this as "a golden age of education [where] there was money and respect and all kinds of things happening."[10]

Teachers who entered education during this First Way and who were still teaching decades later expressed immense nostalgia for the schools of the 1960s and early 1970s. But there were two diametrically opposed nostalgias, not one. Teachers in schools that had been more innovative were nostalgic for the freedom to develop curricula to meet the varying needs of their students as part of a mission to change the world. This group believed that today's reform environment of high-stakes testing and curriculum prescription had stolen this mission from them. They grieved for the passion and creativity that had been taken from their teaching.

Teachers in schools that had been more traditional were also nostalgic for their lost professional autonomy, but not for the same reason. For them, autonomy meant liberty to teach academic subjects just as they chose— including long lectures in which they could display their subject mastery. They remembered schools that were smaller, where unmotivated students left early for employment, and where the students who stayed wanted to learn.

The First Way therefore suffered from huge variations in focus and quality. Whether a school was traditional or innovative, excellent or awful, creative or bland, depended on the lottery of leadership among individual school leaders within an unregulated profession. The theories of change in action during this First Way could start innovation and spread it among a few enthusiasts. However, the skill base of teacher education rested on intuition and ideology, and not on evidence. There was no leadership development to create consistency of impact or effort. Parents had no way of knowing how their children were doing in school beyond the information conveyed on report cards. Fads were adopted uncritically, and many young radicals turned schools upside down during their brief tenures before leaving for greener pastures.

This unevenness in implementation pervaded the First Way and helped erode public trust—not just in education, but in the welfare state itself. Outside education, First Way reforms also fostered long-term dependency and even social exclusion among a hard-core group of recipients who lacked the experience, skills, or dispositions to find employment and succeed in the marketplace. A backlash began. Something had to change.

THE INTERREGNUM OF
COMPLEXITY AND CONTRADICTION

By the mid-1970s, the First Way had reached its limit. The oil crisis that began in 1973 had plunged the world into a recession. An impatient public, demoralized and upset by the war in Vietnam, by the spectacle of long gas lines in America, by power and coal strikes during the United Kingdom's notorious Winter of Discontent (1978–79), and by the expense of ever-expanding bureaucracies, began to question how their tax revenues were being spent. With jobs drying up, welfare claims escalating, and the salaries of teachers and other tenured state professionals increasing with their seniority, education no longer seemed to be effective.

From the mid- 1970s to the late 1980s, an interregnum set in. President Ronald Reagan in the United States and Prime Minister Margaret Thatcher in Britain reduced resources for and infused market principles into the welfare state. They pushed through the full or partial privatization of services and market competition between providers that placed professionals under new pressures to perform. Similar strategies emerged in New Zealand, the Canadian province of Alberta, and the Australian state of Victoria.

At first, the introduction of new market freedoms injected energy and initiative into the state system. The United States saw the emergence of the charter school movement, powered by an unlikely coalition of libertarians, 1960s-inspired antiestablishment activists, and parents of color from the inner cities. Government magnet schools were developed to create achievement opportunities for inner-city youth so they could concentrate on areas of interest in which they excelled. Benefiting from these reforms, one school in the *Change Over Time* study that was designated as a magnet school was transformed from being one of the worst high schools in its city to standing among the top 150 schools in the country.

On the other side of the Atlantic, Thatcher's education minister, Sir Keith Joseph, provoked passionate debates about secondary school reform. Vocational education, long a neglected domain, came alive with new initiatives. Mentoring and tutoring programs for every individual student were the trailblazers of today's personalized learning. The radical idea that high school students should have portfolios of diverse assessments and achievements negotiated and discussed on a continuing basis with a mentor teacher foreshadowed the current growth in assessment-for-learning. Hybrid vocational programs where students attended their home school for the mainstream curriculum in the morning, then moved to another school in their town or city in the afternoon to engage in communications or production technologies according to their interests, anticipated England's current national system of "specialist" secondary schools.

After the inconsistencies of the First Way, this transitional period marked a quest for coherence. Her Majesty's Inspectorate in England defined eight broad areas of educational experience (somewhat similar to Howard Gardner's multiple intelligences) to provide balance, breadth, and coherence in the curriculum.[11] In 1981, the Reagan White House commissioned *A Nation at Risk*, which led to support for common educational standards, along with provision for consumer choice and increased professional training at the district level.[12] Statewide, many governments started to design a common curriculum based on broad standards that were not so numerous as to eliminate professional autonomy or stifle classroom creativity. A little later, the Canadian province of Ontario, under the only socialist government in its history, echoed these emphases by promoting detracking (destreaming) and a small number of common learning outcomes, approached in an interdisciplinary way.[13] In all these cases, leading policymakers believed that the right combination of market pressures, government guidelines, and site-level resources would drive up the quality of teaching, which in turn would raise student achievement.

However, for the classroom teacher on the receiving end of change, this combination of centralized frameworks and initiatives with decentralized responsibility seemed bewilderingly contradictory. Portfolio assessments were paralleled by standardized tests. Interdisciplinary initiatives ran alongside subject-based report cards. Magnet schools targeted to particular populations also had to include populations with special educational needs to meet federal civil rights guidelines.

The more innovative schools had leaders who were able to help teachers interpret the complexity together. They succeeded in maintaining their missions while still addressing the standards. Traditional schools in the *Change Over Time* study, however, drifted into decline as their leaders overprotected their staffs and shielded them from the gathering shadow of Mordor and its reform requirements that threatened the hobbit-like Middle Earth of their schools—until it was too late. Without the guidance of effective leadership, teachers in these schools complained that the outcomes were too vague. Many school districts responded by composing and compiling big binders of highly specific outcomes, but teachers disliked these as well. Frustrated leaders threw up their hands in despair, concluding that teachers are never satisfied! But the answer to outcomes and standards lies not in how they are written or imposed, but in how communities of teachers make sense of them together in relation to the particular students they teach.

In the end, these reforms, like many others, depended for their success on effective leadership, high-quality professional learning, and student engagement with the changes that affected them. But training for existing leaders was nonexistent or discretionary. Most professional development for teachers remained haphazard and workshop driven. No one yet showed confidence in students as agents of reform. The collapse of common understanding and consistent quality was the result of the system's failure to invest in its people.

THE SECOND WAY OF
MARKETS AND STANDARDIZATION

Mounting frustration with years of incoherence and inconsistency, a continuing economic climate of limited public expenditure and overall financial stringency, and the growth of political and parent nostalgia for tradition and certainty helped propel many nations into a strident Second Way of markets and standardization.

In education, the full onslaught of the Second Way arrived earliest in England, Northern Ireland, and Wales in the late 1980s with the launching of detailed and prescriptive national curricula. It emerged a little later, in the early 1990s, in some Australian states. After starting slowly in a small number of U.S. southern states in the 1980s, it exploded in the United States after one of those state governors—Bill Clinton—was elected president in 1992. Ontario also undertook a similar path in the mid-1990s, with Alberta's Conservative government preceding it. Increasingly, the Second Way agenda also came to define the educational reform strategies and conditions of international lending organizations such as the World Bank when change was introduced in developing countries.

In this truly international Second Way, markets were overlaid with growing government centralization and standardization of educational goals. Performance standards and achievement targets enforced political control of outcomes in the public sector. In Australia, Canada, the United Kingdom, and the United States, with lesser or greater degrees of resources and support, this period witnessed the imposition of prescriptive and sometimes punitive reforms in the shape of

- increased competition among schools, fuelled by publication of rankings of test results;
- prescribed, paced, and sometimes scripted curriculum content in areas of learning that were more narrowly defined;
- the misuse of literacy coaches as compliance officers, along with periodic inspections and management walk-throughs to boost skill development and enforce curriculum fidelity;
- political targets and timetables for delivering improved results;

- sanctions such as involuntary teacher transfers, principal removal, and school closure when failure persisted;
- teacher training that moved away from the academy towards on-the-job training in schools; and
- replacement of broad professional learning by in-service training on government priorities.

During the Reagan and Thatcher years, *citizens* were redefined as *clients, customers,* or *consumers.* Facing economic crisis and the salary burdens of maturing state professionals, the welfare state (stigmatized as the "Nanny state" by Thatcher) was demonized as a thief of taxpayers' money. In education, parents who understood how to navigate new provisions for school choice were freed and empowered, but the professionals who served them became subject to greater surveillance and government prescription. The *passive trust* of the First Way when parents respectfully handed their children over to teachers who were left to get on with the job was replaced in the Second Way by an *active mistrust* between parents and teachers.

Some argue that this Second Way promoted a sense of urgency, attended to all students, increased teachers' skill levels, and moved the profession in a common and accountable direction.[14] Equity advocates representing traditionally disenfranchised populations believed that increased accountability measures might even boost and equalize achievement.[15] Others welcomed the new commitment to gathering comprehensive data on student achievement, anticipating that more precise information would lead to greater assistance for struggling students such as those in special education programs and their schools.[16]

However, after the energy and initiative of the interregnum, markets and diversity were quickly trumped by standardization and uniformity. In the United States, statewide high-stakes tests were increasingly administered to all students—even those who were newly arrived from abroad, without the barest rudiments of English. Standards were easy to write and inexpensive to fund; they spread like wildfire. They were revered in administrative and policy circles but resented and resisted in classrooms. However, as scripted and paced literacy programs were then imposed in many districts and on their schools, the bureaucratic screw tightened with increased ferocity.

England lost its local innovative energy in the Second Way, which began when a new national curriculum was imposed in 1988. Standardized achievement tests were subsequently introduced at four age points in 1995, published by rankings in newspapers and on government Web sites, and linked to the feared school inspection agency, Ofsted, which placed schools it judged to be low performing in "Special Measures." When the New Labour government succeeded the Tories in 1997, resources were slowly restored to the system, but there was no letup of top-down pressure. If anything, pressure intensified through the introduction of a timed, prescribed, and paced National Literacy and Numeracy Strategy that was imposed on all primary schools in England. In theory, schools had been given devolved responsibility for budgets and implementation. In practice, the restricted scope for autonomous action amounted in many cases to displacement of blame from governments to schools when results were poor. (See Figure 1.2.)

Meanwhile, in the province of Ontario, the new Progressive Conservative government installed its own detailed secondary school curriculum. The government reduced resources for teachers, mandated a high-stakes Grade 10 literacy test linked to student graduation, and broadcast doubts about teachers' commitments to the public good.

Figure 1.2   The Second Way

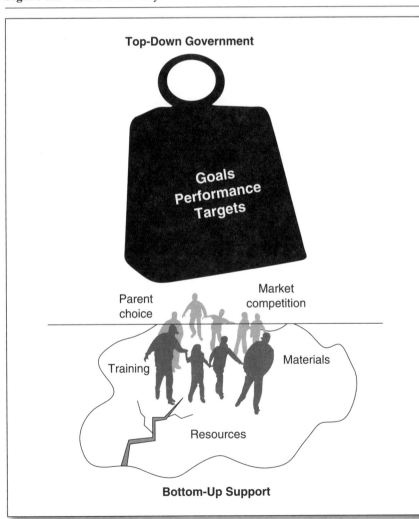

Despite undeniable benefits of clearer focus, greater consistency, and attention to all students with a stronger sense of urgency, the downsides of Second Way reforms were enormous. Achievement gains often occurred for a year or two in most cases but soon reached a plateau.[17] Markets reorganized resources but didn't produce more of them. Parents had more choices, but only the affluent ones knew how to work the system to advance their interests and protect their privileges.[18] Standards raised the bar but didn't help children reach it. As measures of performance rose in tested literacy, rates of reading for pleasure actually fell.[19] The costs to the quality, depth, and breadth of children's learning were considerable. School dropouts increased, site-based innovations declined, teacher quality suffered, and so did teacher retention.[20] Leaders of teachers' professional associations claimed that even if the reforms did yield success, the goals could have been achieved equally well or even better by less professionally punitive means.[21]

The comments of teachers in the *Change Over Time* study on the heyday of this Second Way captured the profession's feelings of fear, frustration, and lost effectiveness that this strategy produced. In U.S. schools, teachers bemoaned the "taking away of professional judgment and autonomy." "There just seems to be so much focus on meeting the standards set from the outside that I don't think we get to spend as much time thinking about what we're going to be doing in the classroom and enjoying it," one said. Though some teachers were "still excited about teaching," others confessed that they couldn't "deal with the system . . . and [were] tired of fighting it."[22]

The impact of the Second Way on professional motivation was just as stark. England experienced a crisis of professional recruitment and retention; 40% of teachers who have completed training are not in the profession after one year.[23] In the United States, 50% of beginning urban teachers have left the profession in the first three years and 50% of all new teachers have left within five years.[24] In Ontario, of the teachers surveyed in six high schools during the era of standardized reform, 85% were more hesitant about seeking a leadership position since the introduction of the reforms, 73% were more motivated to take early retirement, and 78% were less likely to advise their own children to go into teaching.[25]

Whatever impact the Second Way might have had in other social sectors such as health or urban development, in education it precipitated a crisis of sinking professional motivation and lost classroom creativity. As one of the Canadian teachers said in the *Change Over Time* study, "The creativity is gone!"[26] Draconian reforms jacked up short-term gains on state and provincial tests but these did not generalize to other assessments that were immune to test-preparation strategies.[27] The collateral damage on classroom creativity and on curriculum in social studies, health education, and the arts was just too great.[28] A new Way was needed in society and in education to restore professional energy and develop the higher levels of creative learning and skill development essential for competitive and cohesive knowledge societies.

THE THIRD WAY OF
PERFORMANCE AND PARTNERSHIPS

The First Way of educational change offered innovation but no consistency or cohesion. The Second Way enforced greater competition and increased expectations, but at too great a cost to student learning, teacher motivation, and leadership capacity in schools. Enter, then, the Third Way, with its intention to combine the best of state support and market competition.

In 1996, the leadership of the Democratic Party in the United States signed a new declaration that argued for a political approach that could engage with a globalized economy, the end of the Cold War, and the collapse of the big institutions of industry and the state that used to coordinate and control people's lives.[29] The New Democrats surrounding Bill Clinton referred to their new progressivism as "the Third Way," and found common cause with other political leaders seeking to wed 1960s idealism with the on-the-ground challenges of governance. Riding on the wave of a surging economy, the old oppositions between the Right and the Left were put aside for a new political philosophy that was pragmatic, effective, and inspirational.

In Britain, the rebranded New Labour party broadened its base beyond the old working class and the unions, and abolished its commitment to putting the infrastructural industries such as energy and transportation under exclusive state ownership. New Labour didn't want the state to monopolize people's lives but didn't like the threat that unfettered markets posed to social cohesion, either. Their own Third Way therefore emphasized responsibilities as well as rights, being tough on crime as well as on the causes of crime, maintaining social cohesion while stimulating a dynamic economy, and providing stronger support for state professionals at the same time as demanding more accountability from them. Prime Minister Tony Blair and Chancellor Gerhard Schröder wrote a joint policy paper setting out the *both/and* philosophy of the Third Way, and Anthony Giddens gave it theoretical backbone and credibility.[30]

Giddens proposed that the Third Way should go beyond the bureaucracies of the First Way and the cutthroat competition of the Second Way to establish creative combinations of public, private, and voluntary solutions to social problems through what he called "structural pluralism." Finding the right balance of top-down and bottom-up initiatives, as well as partnerships among different public, private, nonprofit, and voluntary providers, he hoped, would promote economic prosperity in inclusive and participatory democracies. This approach included the following:

- *An open state* that is transparent and that empowers citizens through access to public information
- *An efficient and cost-effective government* that delivers value for money through performance targets, auditing, and greater employee participation
- *Public participation* that is more widespread and more vigorous in shaping public policy
- *Community renewal* that invests in and supports self-organization through working with voluntary, charitable, business, and faith-based groups
- *Changes to family policy* so the care of children is a paramount social priority, and rights and responsibilities among parents are distributed more equally
- *A mixed economy* of public and private investment in education and other areas
- A commitment to *greater social inclusion* through equal opportunities to receive quality health care and education, and to participate together in public life
- Understanding that *education cannot achieve everything by itself*, and that economic equalities have to be tackled at their source
- *Reconstructed welfare* that gives people a hand up through training and counseling, rather than through financial handouts
- *A cosmopolitan culture,* able to engage with others while forging a common identity that pulls groups together in the service of ideals beyond themselves
- *Investment in lifelong learning and training,* with portable practices of qualification and more family-friendly employment conditions essential to a flexible workforce and a more self-reliant and autonomous citizenry

Some of what Giddens advocated as the Third Way has become embedded in an increasingly popular approach to social policy known as "New Public Management."[31] The significantly new element of New Public Management is neither top down nor bottom up, but rather side to side.[32] In New Public Management, a lot of the energy for change comes from the public and the professions. Greater consumer responsiveness and increased public investment in families and children's services are designed to increase public engagement with and participation in the development as well as the implementation of policy. Funding and support for more professional development, better leadership training, and the creation of professional networks geared towards improvement are established to offset the deficits of professional motivation that the punitive, top-down approach of the Second Way had created.

In the New Public Management version of the Third Way, government establishes specific goals—such as the closely specified "Adequate Yearly Progress" indicators in the United States or systemwide literacy targets in England and in Ontario—and provides greater oversight at every level. League tables printed in newspapers and digital media inform the public about student achievement results; parents in underachieving schools are given opportunities to transfer their children to schools that have better results. Educators are encouraged to build lateral learning networks to drive change and the public has access to information about teacher quality and student achievement levels. The government sponsors outsourcing of some educational provisions, such as the "supplementary educational services" provided by NCLB, to students in struggling schools. "Diverse provider models" enable parents and students to shop among a variety of school options. In the United Kingdom, leading soccer clubs work in partnership with local authorities to establish and run learning centers where underachieving children, especially boys, can be switched on to learning through sport.[33] Visually, the Third Way is represented in Figure 1.3.

Figure 1.3   The Third Way

Many Third Way policies have been realized—and across party and political lines. On both sides of the Atlantic, Democratic and Labour governments have accepted arguments of their former adversaries and injected market principles into welfare state programs related to education, health care, and public housing. Even rock-ribbed conservatives such as George W. Bush dramatically increased expenditure on education.

THIRD WAY SYSTEMS

In spite of increased allocations, however, there were only the faintest glimmerings of the Third Way in the U.S. educational system during George W. Bush's two presidential terms. In the United States, the Second Way still reigned supreme. At the time this book was sent to press—spring 2009—President Barack Obama was making the reform of U.S. education a cornerstone of his administration. Given this delayed acknowledgment by U.S. policymakers of the need to move beyond the Second Way, it is essential to consider developments in places such as Britain and parts of Canada where the Third Way has already established a firm footing.

England

In England, the Third Way is evident in top-down measures that emphasize performance targets for schools and school districts. Indicators are gathered from tests in literacy, numeracy, and science at four (now three) age points or key stages from age seven; in a wide range of examination results at age 16 (the key measure being collecting five passes at Grade C or above); and now in other areas, too, such as students' well-being. A streamlined system of inspection of schools by the government's inspection agency, Ofsted, relies heavily on prior access to published achievement data because it keeps schools focused on making measurable improvement. Moreover, National Literacy and Numeracy hours of timed, paced, and initially scripted instruction ensure primary schools concentrate on these core areas. As a consequence, England's system of bureaucratic and political pressure has been "hard as nails," in the words of one of its chief architects, always ready for the "naming and shaming" of its struggling schools.[34] In some respects, these policies have been even stricter than in the previous Second Way of markets and standardization, although now degrees of intervention are related inversely to levels of school success.

In tune with the Third Way, England's New Labour government also provided extensive training and quality materials for its literacy and numeracy strategy. It reduced class sizes and put droves of support staff into schools to relieve teachers from extraneous administrative tasks and other workload pressures.[35] The *Building Schools for the Future* initiative established a 10-year program of building new secondary schools, some of them located in the country's most economically depressed and racially divided towns and cities.[36] A successful *Sure Start* program has given more children, especially from poor families, an earlier start and educational opportunities. Partnerships with businesses, universities, and community organizations have led to the creation of brand-new secondary school academies in many inner cities where their educational predecessors had been failing. And the founding of the world's first National College for School Leadership has increased the priority and prestige of educational leadership as a central part of both capacity-building and change-management strategies in the system. This bounty of funded activity sets the Third Way apart from its more-market-driven and under-resourced predecessor.

Finally, publication of more and more amounts and kinds of performance data has increased the information available to parents when they choose their children's school. Integration of education with children's services at national and local levels has been designed to connect schools more to their communities and to give coordinated attention to the whole child's development. All kinds of incentives have been offered to teachers and schools to network with and learn from their peers, especially in terms of successful schools taking on or even taking over weaker partners as a way to drive up standards.

Ontario

The Canadian province of Ontario represents an even more advanced version of Third Way thinking. In the latter half of the 1990s, the province was the epitome of Second Way standardization. Its conservative agenda of diminished resources and reductions in teachers' preparation time, high-stakes tests linked to graduation, and accelerating reform requirements exacted high costs on teaching and learning. Teachers in the *Change Over Time* study complained of there being "too many changes, too fast," "too much, too quickly," "just so much, so soon," to an extent that was "too vast and just overwhelming." Having to "take shortcuts" meant that teachers did not "always feel [they] could do [their] best work." "What a waste of my intelligence, creativity, and leadership potential!" one teacher concluded.[37] Ontario's educational system was as far removed from the needs of a fast-paced, flexible knowledge economy as it is possible to get.

This changed in 2003, when the Liberal Party of Premier Dalton McGuinty took office. McGuinty made two inspired appointments: recruiting educational policy scholar Ben Levin to the education ministry's most senior position, and international educational reform expert Michael Fullan to serve as his own educational change advisor. The province then set upon a new course by reversing many previous policies and wedding a continuing and ever-escalating commitment to test-based educational accountability with a range of initiatives that built capacity for improvement and provided professional support.[38]

From England, Ontario borrowed the idea of creating a Literacy and Numeracy Secretariat as the centerpiece of a guiding government coalition that could steer the reforms through. In addition to the existing testing system, set up and maintained by the previous conservative and socialist governments, McGuinty's party also imported England's idea of top-down, political, systemwide targets for improved performance in literacy and numeracy within one election term.[39]

In true Third Way fashion, these top-down measures were paralleled by and combined with extensive bottom-up and lateral supports. Thousands of new teaching positions were created to reduce class sizes to a maximum of 20 in the primary grades. In addition, "student success teachers" were designated in every high school to ensure that each student would be well known and supported by at least one school staff member. The Literacy and Numeracy Secretariat drove the improvement of instruction by large teams of consultants and coaches working in schools in conjunction with the support of quality materials. While the provincial performance targets are fixed, schools and districts are also encouraged to commit to and set their own targets.

Within a framework of high aspirations, Ontario has placed a considerable emphasis on capacity building. The teachers' unions have been allocated $5 million to spend on professional development. Successful practices are networked across schools. Underperforming schools are encouraged but not compelled to seek assistance from government support teams and higher-achieving peers when their performance sags. Changing up, down, and across, Ontario is arguably the most sophisticated Third Way system of educational reform in existence.

The United States

The United States barely embarked on the Third Way during the first years of the 21st century. The federal government remained resolutely stuck in the rut of failed Second Way solutions. Despite its urgent insistence on improvement and equity, NCLB legislation, alongside endless and contradictory systems of statewide and districtwide testing, had narrowed and dumbed down the curriculum. Anachronistic Second Way policies had given schools multiple and contradictory ways to fail, removed creativity from the classroom, and precipitated crises of retention in teaching and leadership. Unrealistic change timelines, draconian intervention strategies that included principal removal and school closure, accelerated carousels of leadership turnover, and ceaseless exposures of and emphases on failure all epitomized the punitive pressures of top-down, Second Way reforms.

The promised support of full funding for NCLB was never honored by President George W. Bush; Senator Ted Kennedy, cosponsor of the Act, pointedly boycotted its first anniversary celebration at the White House. Subsequent economic developments led many tax-starved school districts to withdraw literacy coaches and other key personnel as the credit crunch hit, thereby making the kinds of lateral learning promoted in Canada and England much more difficult to achieve. The funding offered to schools, when it did come, came in dribs and drabs, arriving with the attached strings of impossible improvement deadlines that produced panic-driven measures of short-term change. Strategies for professionals to work with colleagues across or beyond the confinements of their own districts were almost entirely absent.

There were some bursts of creativity in the United States during the years when England and Canada were advancing into the Third Way, but these almost all came from outside government. Former high-profile advocates of the Second Way, including two previous U.S. secretaries of education, reversed course and argued that educational systems must encourage the innovation and creativity needed to compete in a global knowledge economy.[40] In cities such as Boston, Denver, New York, and Philadelphia, clusters of traditional public schools, charter schools, and various hybrids such as pilot schools found ways to share coaches and mentors and were given greater autonomy to innovate in exchange for producing better results.[41] Long lists of students waiting to get into alternative schools that had proven successful testified to the attractiveness of many of the start-ups for those burned out by unresponsive bureaucracies.

In the absence of federal leadership during the Bush administration, foundations played a more central role in the United States than in England or Canada. The Bill and Melinda Gates Foundation invested in converting high school behemoths into more intimate and more personalized learning communities.[42] The Wallace Foundation tried to turn principals into leaders rather than mere managers.[43] Other foundations and venture capital organizations, such as the New Schools Venture Fund, helped teachers and schools to use achievement data as a basis for improvement and intervention decisions.[44]

The Obama presidency is encouraging a new climate for educational change that shows signs of building on these earlier initiatives. There is not merely talk of more educational innovation but also now a new federal agency to promote it. Better tests and assessments such as growth rather than status models are being called for that will measure higher-level knowledge and skills beyond the basics that dominate many existing statewide instruments. A willingness to address the influence of out-of-school factors on children's learning and well-being as in the wraparound services of the Harlem Children's Zone indicates a dramatic departure from previous policies.

From the very beginning, Third Way strategies have been transported back and forth across national boundaries. Sir Michael Barber, who designed and oversaw the delivery systems in 10 Downing Street for much of England's Third Way, supplied advice on New York City's reforms under Chancellor Joel Klein and now is working with a consortium of U.S. state governors. Ontario's Michael Fullan is advising a number of U.S. states on their strategies, too. The Third Way will clearly be a part of the U.S. policy agenda for years to come.

CONCLUSION

Third Way advocates have sought to address the dawning realization that education in the 21st century must move beyond the control of self-serving professionals under freewheeling progressivism and beyond the dark thicket of prescription and standardization that limits capacity and stifles initiative. Their vision is a broad and generous one that reconciles and harmonizes the major political rifts that have divided Democrats and Republicans in the United States and Labour and Tories in the United Kingdom. A blend of top-down control, bottom-up initiative, and sophisticated lateral learning, they hope, will prepare leading Western democracies to thrive in the new knowledge societies of the future.

In terms of ultimate social goals—public and civic engagement, professional learning, and the most rigorous standards of academic achievement—we stand squarely with Third Way educational advocates such as Michael Fullan and Sir Michael Barber. System leaders eager to move beyond unimaginative models of reform have much to learn from them.

But there is a crucial difference between our perspective and that of these other change advocates. Not everything that has occurred in the Third Way of educational reform is positive, and some of it is actually problematic. Those who most advertise their own reforms are least likely to broadcast their drawbacks. Unless we are aware of the limitations as well as the strengths of these Third Way reform examples, hasty efforts to import their designs into other states or countries may mean we end up stealing skeletons from other people's closets.

Our accumulating evidence and experience has brought us to the view that, in practice, *the educational reform strategies of the Third Way have distracted its founders and followers from their ability to achieve the Way's original ideals.* The next chapter describes the *three paths of distraction* that have betrayed the Third Way's promise and that have diverted educators and policymakers from its admirable ends. The rest of the book then shows how to deal with the distracters and embark on a new *Fourth Way* of educational change that can deepen learning, raise standards, reduce the differences in achievement, and build a more creative and cohesive future for us all.

The managerially minded almost
always opt for today.
They can only be certain to have
power in the present.
Managers fear the past and the future
and are terrified by the idea of a
combination of the two.

—JOHN RALSTON SAUL
A FAIR COUNTRY, 2008, p. 25

CHAPTER TWO

THE THREE PATHS
OF DISTRACTION

The Path of Autocracy

The Path of Technocracy

The Path of Effervescence

Those things that many use to divide us can also bring us together. The Third Way has offered integrated strategies in a polarized world. By doing so, it has brought into being one of the 10 "megatrends" predicted by John Naisbitt for the 21st century—the replacement of *either/or* thinking with *both/and* solutions. Pressure *and* support, top-down leadership *and* bottom-up empowerment, public *and* private sectors, autonomy *with* accountability—these are just some of the Third Way's creative combinations.[1]

This antipathy to *either/or* thinking isn't new. In education, it's the hallmark of the foundational philosophy of one of America's greatest educators—John Dewey. Dewey disliked the polarized fads and fashions that moved educational policy from one extreme to the other. "Mankind likes to think in terms of extreme opposites," he complained. "It is given to formulating its beliefs in terms of *Either-Ors*, between which it recognizes no intermediate possibilities."[2] To overcome this predisposition towards what he called "dualistic" thinking, Dewey organized many of the chapters of his magnum opus, *Democracy and Education*, to explore synthetic and integrative approaches to learning—"Interest *and* Discipline," "Play *and* Work in the Curriculum," and "Labor *and* Leisure" among them.[3]

Dewey's lectures resonated with educators. *Both/and* thinking is common sense for most teachers. They have no need for the purity or precision of administrators' plans. Plans are rarely perfect in practice, and most are discarded the moment power changes hands. In schools, the only justifiable place for a pendulum is the science lab!

- *Phonics or whole language?* Actually, you need *both* in a program of balanced literacy that reaches all students and the different ways they learn best.
- *Rigor or relevance?* Teachers know that inspired children whose learning connects with their dreams *and* their lives are the most likely to push themselves to higher levels of achievement.
- *Heroic or distributed leadership?* The most charismatic leaders are those who inspire their communities to lead improvement *themselves.*
- *Improvisation or memorization?* In mathematics, music, or drama, there are times to solve problems or create things anew, and times to just grind out the multiplication tables or memorize the score or the script. "To everything there is a season," and most classrooms are like springtime in New England—you can and do get all seasons in one day.

The social theory of the Third Way argued for integrative thinking—linking the best of government leadership with innovative markets in educational change. In practice, though, many Third Way policies have drifted from the Way's original ideals—alienating students, corrupting classrooms, manipulating educators, and deceiving the public. How has this happened?

In *Turnaround Leadership*, Michael Fullan describes how, with his advice, the province of Ontario developed its reform strategy in education. One of the key components was to manage "the distracters," defined as "anything that takes you away from continuous focus on teaching and learning and student achievement."[4] One "big distracter" was union and labor strife inherited from the previous conservative government and its Second Way strategies. This was resolved by signing an agreement with the unions for a period of peace and stability in which improved pay and working conditions were traded for union commitment to the reform agenda. Other distracters involved excessive paperwork and administrative duties imposed on teachers and principals.

Removing distracters like these is invaluable, but government itself can also distract us from positive change. Its political agenda—driven by other concerns, as well as strictly educational ones often assembled by individuals with scant knowledge of the real workings of teaching and schools—sometimes distract people from the path of learning and improvement for all students that many so passionately want to follow.

Consider the case of California, the world's eighth largest economy. The state's antiquated funding system had produced vast disparities among schools in the richest and poorest districts. From 2000 to 2004, a group of plaintiffs from community organizations advised by university experts successfully sued the state to remedy the inequities. Shortly afterwards, however, the state removed billions from the education budget. It required a teacher's union, the California Teachers Association (CTA), to take Governor Schwarzenegger to task by suing him for failing to provide opportunities for students in the state's lowest-performing schools to learn. Having won the lawsuit, the union is now responsible for helping raise achievement in those schools over a seven-year period through the new Quality Investment in Education Act (QIEA). This act provides $2.9 billion to assist 488 struggling schools, identified by a broad range of criteria on the state's Academic Performance Index. Governments don't just deal with distracters: They sometimes create them. When that happens, a socially engaged public and profession has to rectify matters.

Three distinct political paths have distracted and diverted educators and school reformers from the original ideals of the Third Way:

- the *Path of Autocracy*,
- the *Path of Technocracy*, and
- the *Path of Effervescence*.

These paths have intertwined to seduce teachers, students, parents, and reformers away from a straighter, bolder course that is educationally authentic, professionally engaging, democratically empowering, and organizationally sustainable. Taken together, they define a widespread *New Orthodoxy* of educational change that is a far cry from the original vision and promise of the Third Way—especially in relation to that Way's principles of professional and public engagement.

THE PATH OF AUTOCRACY

An autocratic system is one of dictatorial rule exercised through absolute power. In the New Orthodoxy, while the Path of the Autocracy acknowledges that new challenges are emerging, including the need for a more innovative school system and economy, its adherents don't want to give up political control. So, while the Third Way was meant to be a strategy of *development*, it has actually turned into a slickly spun system of top-down *delivery*.

Two highly influential reports represent this Path of Autocracy in near-perfect form. The first—*Tough Choices or Tough Times*—was signed by more than two dozen leading American educators and policymakers as part of the New Commission on the Skills of the American Workforce.[5] Its tone is unabashedly apocalyptic. The Commission launched a blistering assault on the inability of the nation's underperforming and inflexible public education system to develop the innovation and creativity needed in the contemporary global economy. It highlighted America's declining educational performance compared with other industrial nations. The reasons for the decline, the Commission argued, are

- the educational consequences of widening income and wealth disparities between rich and poor;
- delayed starts and interventions for children who most need the strongest support;
- insufficient attention to adult literacy and continuing education for those already in the workforce;
- easy courses and mediocre expectations, especially of adolescents;
- excessive bureaucratic regulation;
- an overreliance on the testing of basic skills to the detriment of creativity and critical thinking;
- a leveling off in recent gains in tested achievement;
- the relatively poor quality of a teaching force drawn from the middle-to-low ranks of college graduates; and
- inflexible and ineffective systems of teacher compensation.

After years of unrelenting standardization in U.S. education, this diagnosis is a breath of fresh air. The quest for creativity, the attack on existing forms of testing, the clarion call for highly qualified teachers, the acknowledgment of income gaps and poverty traps, and the recognition that existing strategies are simply stuck—this is brave, bold, and long-overdue policy thinking. In its assaults on inappropriate assessments in particular, the report must have been sweet music to the ears of worn-down, unappreciated teachers who yearn to return passion and imagination to their teaching.

The description of the problems makes sense. The proposed solutions do not. Part of the explanation for this lies in the Commission's selective use of international evidence. Only 2 of the 13 sidebar exemplars in the report come from outside the United States. There is no reference to the Netherlands—the nation at the top of UNICEF's 2007 survey of child well-being—and its moves towards curriculum decentralization.[6] Nor is there any discussion of high-performing Finland and its commitment to local curriculum development. China's promotion of more school-developed curricula and even England's easing of its National Curriculum requirements are strikingly absent.

Instead of these decentralizing reforms that seek to develop schools as sustainable learning communities, the Commission recommends *more* centralized curriculum mandates for teachers (albeit with content of greater breadth and creativity) and *longer* hours of *harder* work with more demanding exit examinations for students. There will be more market choice and competition and struggles for supremacy and survival between different types of schools and *more* competitive systems of performance-based pay for teachers. Everything should change, it seems, except the increasingly unholy trinity of markets, testing, and accountability. Tough choices, indeed! The new globalized economy, it seems, is going to be driven by a less-than-happy band of Puritans!

Which top-performing nations on international tests have endorsed these standardized and market-driven solutions? Singapore? Finland? The Netherlands? No chance! *The Third Way's Path of Autocracy is about ingrained ideology, not about learning from the evidence of people's successes elsewhere.*

An equally significant report that embraces the same New Orthodoxy is McKinsey & Company's widely publicized report, "How the World's Best-Performing School Systems Come Out on Top."[7] Again, its chief findings seem plausible enough. Get "the right people to become teachers," develop "them into effective instructors," and make certain "the system is able to deliver the best possible instruction for every child." A closer look, however, reveals the same skewed interpretation of international evidence, the same endorsement of testing and accountability, and continuing support and preference for solutions of the now failed free market.

Take the first "driver" of change: getting the "right people" to become teachers. Who can quarrel with that? Everyone wants the smartest, most personable individuals to become their children's teachers. But despite fleeting and flirtatious references to the Finnish exception, it is teachers' performance at raising scores, a system characterized by "set expectations," and a language of delivery and "driven-ness" that dominates its arguments in the report's conclusions. The best systems, we are told, reasonably enough, "all place a strong focus on numeracy and literacy in the early years," "align standards globally, particularly in reference to those of the OECD's PISA [*Programme for International Student Assessment]* assessments and other leading school assessment systems," and "match current teaching to the country's future requirements."[8] The best systems have teachers who are "constantly evaluating student performance and constructing interventions" and have separated teachers' judgments about their collective professional efficacy from those of outsiders who provide "frequent external review."[9]

Only through a careful reading of the fine print, though, can one infer that other forces are being brought into play and given prominence in assessing teacher quality. For example, a small chart on page 17 of the McKinsey & Company report acknowledges that teacher candidates in Finland are checked for their "emotional intelligence" in working with youngsters. Yet aside from one brief boxed-frame reference to emotional intelligence, there is virtually no other discussion of interpersonal skills and dispositions required by talented teachers throughout the report. In discourse analysis, this strategy is known as inoculation: give readers a tiny dose of your opponents' position so that you can ignore or dismiss the rest of it, and your own emphases can prevail. Thus, there is no reference to the inspiring South African philosophy of Ubuntu that asks people to address their own and others' humanity in order to help the community improve, and no reference to the cooperation that characterizes Japanese classrooms and workplaces, nor to the kinds of creativity that are prized by the high-performing start-ups in information technology today and that run throughout the Finnish system. It matters, as McKinsey points out, that the educational system is connected to the society's goals. Of course! Presidents, prime ministers, and premiers of democracies understand that—but so too did Hitler and Mussolini. It matters greatly *what those goals actually are.*

In *real* schools in *real* communities, educational leaders consider a wide variety of factors in putting together a talented teaching staff. A diverse immigrant community needs a cluster of teachers who can speak the language used by many parents and students. Every school has to have at least one technophile to avert system failures and nervous breakdowns. Schools in challenging circumstances also need colleagues with the street smarts and insider knowledge who know how to work with the most dis-affected youth. Pack your building with teachers who have a single-minded focus on raising test scores in the basics and you don't have a learning organization, but rather an ingrained distraction from the core tasks of teaching and learning in a diverse community setting.

In many ways, McKinsey & Company's report reads like a rational-ization of the stalled Third Way strategies of England. Indeed, one of the report's leading authors, Sir Michael Barber, senior advisor on policy delivery to Prime Minister Tony Blair, presided over a micromanaged literacy and numeracy strategy, an intrusive inspection system, and endless rounds of targets and testing. There was more support of money and materials for teachers and more lateral learning across schools, but mainly around meet-ing narrowly defined achievement targets, and rarely around deeper issues of teaching and learning. "Deliverology," in Barber's terms, was the order of the day—not the development of students' learning or teachers' capacity.[10]

Even today, there is little letup. Every time English schools look like they might be reaching the bar set by the government, the government finds a way to redefine what counts as success, so many schools simply fall short of the bar again. When many secondary schools in very poor communities significantly increased the percentage of passes that students gained in the high-stakes General Certificate of Secondary Education (GCSE) exams, the government plunged 638 of these schools straight back into the failure zone by insisting these percentages must always include mathematics and English, and by raising the "pass" bar from 25% to 30%. In this National Challenge, schools that do not turn around within a year will be renamed and remade as newly constituted academies, established with the support of business partners who also exercise high degrees of influence through representation in governance.[11] Alternatively, the schools could be closed altogether. Whenever a school gets close to the bar, the English system simply drops the floor, manufacturing the exaggerated appearances of failure that justify its control and intervention—to the utter exasperation of educators.

Ironically, Barber began his tenure with a Third Way promise of lateral learning. He specifically targeted "short termism," "getting in the way," and "changing the goalposts" as strategies to avoid.[12] But power changes people, as he readily acknowledges. Once in power, "naming and shaming" struggling schools became "decisive both practically and symbolically." The message was that "New Labour would be as hard as nails" with the consequence that—in Barber's own words—"a degree of disillusionment that never fully evaporated set in."[13]

Given this inevitable reaction to the heavy exercise of government power over and against schools, Barber later conceded that, in practice, he had "become associated with the top-down approach to reform which . . . became unfashionable," "while the idea of 'letting go' took hold."[14] Instead, from his perspective, political targets provide a legitimate focus for improvement. For Barber, it is simply other people's problem if they treat the targets as the be-all and end-all of their job. The top-down policies of his delivery unit were always right—they just could have been communicated better "to sustain the same messages for longer" with "fewer distractions" using "more intermediaries" such as school leaders, in a climate of "constant, genuine interaction."[15] Indeed, he reflects, given a second chance, he would do it again—with even greater tenacity.[16] Moreover, Ontario's Third Way government, with its own target-driven reforms, has cited Barber's resolute stance in support of its own rationale for a steadfast approach to educational reform.[17]

In the Path of Autocracy, "letting go" is seen as a sign of weakness, a kind of moral incontinence. Stopping to think, gathering others' opinions, and making midcourse adjustments are viewed as reprehensible failures to hold fast or get a grip when faced with doubt or difficulty.

In her work on "the power of mindful learning," Ellen Langer tells us that excessive rigidity can prevent us from apprehending new information that could lead us to revise our thinking and reconsider not just our strategies but also our previously established goals.[18] A distinguished tradition of work on organizational learning yields the same result. Double-loop learning that provides constant feedback allows organizations to evolve and improve continuously, compared with single-loop learning that leaves existing norms and values unchallenged.[19] Being driven only by intended outcomes, rather than also being open to new information as it emerges, can lead to an enervating "mindlessness" that promotes habit, ritual, and compliance rather than learning, creativity, and change.

In reality, "letting go" is essential to highly skilled performance. In his incisive analysis of high-quality craftsmanship in carpentry, cooking, music, and sport, American sociologist Richard Sennett points to the virtues of "minimum force" and the art of "release."

> If the cook, like a carpenter, holds the cleaver or hammer down after striking a blow, it works against the tool's rebound. . . . The ability to withdraw force in the microsecond after it is applied also makes the gesture itself more precise; one's aim improves. So it is in playing the piano where the ability to release a key is an integral motion with pressing it down. Finger pressure must cease at the moment of contact for the fingers to move easily and swiftly to other keys. In playing stringed instruments, as we go to a new tone, our hand can make the move cleanly only by letting go, a microsecond before, of the string it has pressed before. In the musical hand, for this reason, it is harder to produce a clear, soft sound than to belt out loud notes.[20]

These principles of letting go or failing to do so, writes Sennett, apply equally well to political and military strategists. "Brute force" is as counterproductive in leadership and "state-craft" as it is in any other craft. Instead, "cooperation with the weak, restrained force [and] release after attack" are essential to the artistry of effective political control."[21] It is the strongest—those who have greater muscular or mental control—who can let go most effectively. When leaders refuse to "let go" at the right moment, it is not strength they display, but rigidity.

Policy exponents of the New Orthodoxy have not been able to get beyond "belting out loud notes" through the unrestrained hammer blows of heavy-handed government interventions into districts and schools. In policy and administration, it is time to play a different tune, and with more accomplished virtuosity.

THE PATH OF TECHNOCRACY

Autocrats have little time for artistry. Technocrats have even less time for it. In Florian Henckel von Donnersmarck's fascinating 2007 film, *The Lives of Others*, communist East Berlin in the 1980s is the setting for the secret police's bugging of the apartment of one of the country's leading playwrights.[22] In this ultimate surveillance society, the state collects and counts data in voluminous, hand-sorted files about the activities of its subjects—letters received, newspapers taken, shoes purchased, and the times of arrival in and departure from the apartment. The only statistics not collected are those that are inconvenient for the government—for instance, those that draw attention to the country's suicide rates. In this society, data are not collected episodically, but continuously, in the event that a case might need to be prosecuted at some point in the future. In this manner, all of the "objective," wide-ranging, intrusive evidence will be at hand for the state to exercise its control and judgment over its subjects. In this world, the emotionless technocrat holds the levers of control, while the expressive and disturbing artist is his enemy.

The Third Way started with the promise of equity, public engagement, and economic prosperity. But in education a second distracter—the Path of Technocracy—has converted moral issues of inequality and social justice that should be a shared social responsibility into technical calculations of student progress targets and achievement gaps that are confined to the school. Achievement gaps reflect economic and social status gaps that exist around the world. Increasingly, though, teachers and schools have been made solely accountable for the persistence of these gaps. Moral issues and responsibilities are converted into technical issues and responsibilities to be resolved through ever-increasing testing and analysis of voluminous amounts of numerical achievement data. Evidence is not only collected about people, but individuals are also increasingly required to collect data about themselves and each other to check and chart their progress on a never-ending basis.

But hang on a moment! Isn't it a bit extreme to liken Anglo-Saxon educational change strategies to the pervasive spying of communist Berlin? Is collecting better data and using it intelligently really all that sinister or bad? Isn't the gathering of data a cornerstone of the scientific method, a method that just has not been applied properly to teaching and schools in the past?

In education today, data are collected on student and teacher performance, school performance, the system's performance on examination results, standardized test scores, attendance and absenteeism rates, and now also on a range of indicators of student well-being. Should we be all that concerned?

- More and more individual students have the right and the responsibility to meet with their teacher, mentor, or progress manager every few weeks to review their scores together and see where more effort or intervention might be needed. *Doesn't this finally give students an active voice in their own learning?*
- Schools can be clearer about where their problems are—a weak department here, an underperforming group of boys in reading there—so they can focus their interventions and assistance more precisely. *Doesn't this give help to those who most need it, and stop teachers from scattering their efforts to the winds?*
- Teachers can be recognized and rewarded for the difference they make to the students they teach over the course of a school year, in terms of measures of value-added achievement. *Isn't this more objective, appropriate, and fair than paying people according to their seniority or administrative responsibilities?*
- Higher- and lower-performing schools and teachers serving similar kinds of students can be identified openly so schools can be connected to peers who can help them and parents can become better informed about what's going on. *Doesn't this encourage and support people to help them improve together?*
- Classroom pedagogy can be based on clear and objective evidence of what works in relation to student achievement instead of on the basis of instinct, ideology, intuition, or habit. *If teachers want to be treated as real professionals, shouldn't they act more like doctors and base their practice on hard evidence rather than on personal preference or unexamined belief?*
- Professional learning communities of teachers and leaders can look at performance data together to face up to their problems, find shared solutions, and engage in invigorating professional conversations about how to improve practice. *Haven't teachers complained for years about getting too little praise and feedback, and about having to work in lonely conditions of classroom isolation?*

Few could deny the importance of data in the information age. In physical examinations, financial forecasting, and air traffic control systems, we can't operate or even survive without data. In education, data can and do inform our decisions, stimulate professional conversation, prick our consciences, monitor progress, and force us to face our responsibilities and confront our shortcomings. When teachers have data they can use quickly to adjust their teaching, and when they understand the strengths and limitations of those data, then schools can become better learning organizations and everyone can prosper.

In the New Orthodoxy, though, something else has happened. Exorbitant promises have been made about what the data can do. Data are sometimes discrepant and don't appear to agree. Data might relate to standards that teachers don't value. Statistical data aren't always self-evident: Professional judgment and experience are needed to interpret and add other information to them. The problem with the Path of Technocracy is not that it's loaded with data, but with

- how data and evidence have come to be *defined and delimited,*
- how data are *interpreted and used,* and
- how *overreliance on data distorts the system* and leads it to ignore and marginalize the importance of moral judgment and professional responsibility.

1. MISLEADING DATA

In schools and school systems, the data of the New Orthodoxy mostly come down to standardized test scores in literacy and mathematics, and sometimes in science. Technocrats value what they measure instead of measuring what they value. They narrow the curriculum, prioritize the tested basics, and turn a blind eye to teaching to the test. Because tests vary between districts, states, and nations, schools can frustratingly find themselves performing well on one test and catastrophically on another—as when more than 300 schools in California met the state's goals for student achievement gains but failed to make "Adequate Yearly Progress" as defined by the No Child Left Behind Act (NCLB).[23]

There are also inconsistencies and contradictions over time, such as the squadron of 638 newly failing secondary schools in England's National Challenge. Those schools that score well under one year's exam or test criteria may miss the target the following year when the government moves the goal posts.[24] Another example is when schools are given no time for a trial run to develop their skills when a new test or reform is introduced. The result is that the baseline results are artificially depressed (just as the later gains for which governments claim credit are really no more than a recovery).

One popular response to these objections is "value-added assessments" —more-sophisticated measures of what difference a teacher makes to a class of students' achievement, or what difference a school makes to a grade cohort of students over one year or more. One of the most influential versions of this approach is the value-added model (VAM) pioneered by William Sanders, a previously obscure agricultural statistician at the University of Tennessee at Knoxville. Starting in the 1990s, Sanders applied what he called the "Tennessee Value-Added Assessment System" to students taking Tennessee's standardized tests at the beginning and end of each school year. Using computational algorithms that he has never made public, Sanders was able to show how students entering a classroom at the same level could make striking gains or even regress over multiple years based on the quality of teachers to whom they were assigned.[25] Here was a way to identify truly high-quality teachers and to protect teachers from being blamed for the learning deficits that students brought with them to a classroom at the beginning of the year. By 2008, more than 50 districts were rewarding teacher performance with bonuses and raises based on value-added models. At last, the wheat could be separated from the chaff.

Yet, puzzlingly, from a statistical standpoint, one year's wheat often turns out to be next year's chaff. In their rigorous quantitative study of four school districts using VAM in Florida from 2001 to 2005, Daniel McCaffrey and his colleagues found that, at best, slightly less than half (47%) of the teachers in the top quintile stayed in that category from one year to the next. In two of the four districts, the figure was less than a quarter.[26] These results were comparable to previous studies conducted in San Diego and Chicago. "In general," the authors observe, "about one-third of teachers ranked in the top 20 percent one year are also ranked in the top quintile the following year."[27]

So what happened? Were teachers brilliant one year, but then forgot everything they knew the next? The hard truth is that while a small number of teachers are able to generate consistently high outcomes across years, in most cases there is lots of movement up and down from one year to the next. Every experienced teacher and school administrator knows why. Teachers and students have good years and bad. People get sick, a parent dies, a marriage breaks up, or a teacher loses sleep after the new baby arrives. An inspiring principal leaves and an underwhelming successor follows. Just *one* child with extreme behavior difficulties can disrupt an entire class and wreck results. Figuring out the intricacies of a new mandated curriculum initiative can lead to a dip in students' test scores, only to have them bounce back in subsequent years when the teacher masters the material.

Got cancer? Had a baby? Lost your dad? Took on a difficult student? Risked making a big change to learn how to teach a new curriculum? Congratulations—we'll pay you less! And no complaining, because we've got a new data-driven decision-making system to back us up!

We have seen all this and more in our own research. In one study, we evaluated a network of 300 secondary schools that had been designated as underachieving by the government.[28] Two-thirds of the schools improved dramatically over one to two years. But our site visits revealed that while many turnarounds were the result of the project's intervention, others were due to different factors entirely. One school was designated as underperforming during the year in which the wife of the principal died, and then rebounded when the principal recovered by throwing himself into his work. Another had a perfect storm of crises—including accusations of a police officer having raped a student—that distracted everyone's attention until the case was resolved and student learning once again became the focus of teachers and school leaders.

These humble and human dilemmas of *real* life in *real* schools and communities fly under the technocrat's radar. On the path of technocracy, data are defined and operationalized narrowly, simplistically, and unthinkingly. Computer data are trusted. Teachers' judgments are not!

2. MISINTERPRETED DATA

In industry, evidence about quality often seems obvious. A component either fits or it doesn't. The measurements are either correct or they're not. Even here, though, the reasons for the defect are not always obvious. Could it be a problem with raw materials and the supply chain? Is the workmanship deficient? Is the workforce unskilled, poorly supervised, or even actively engaged in sabotage? If so, why? When data point to deficits, good managers don't leap to conclusions and respond impulsively. Instead, they ask "Why?" and include others in the inquiry with them.

But what about medicine—the gold standard for evidence-based improvement? Or what about high-stakes professional sports, where demanding fans insist on nothing other than a winning score? Surely educators can learn something from them about crunching the numbers correctly?

Atul Gawande is a general surgeon at the Brigham and Women's Hospital in Boston. He is also a best-selling medical writer and a regular contributor to *The New Yorker*. He has written two prominent books on medical issues that advance a sophisticated understanding of the relationship between evidence and experience. Gawande has explored the mysteries and fallibilities of medicine in the cases of

- a hernia center that is highly effective because of years of specialization and practice;
- an outstanding cystic fibrosis unit that gets astonishing success rates not because of more stringent evidence-based procedures, but because its highly experienced doctors exercise intuitive judgments in their rich interactions with patients; and
- the case of a woman Gawande spared from a potentially fatal flesh-eating disease when he and a trusted colleague decided to operate

after they allowed their intuition to override all the objective tests that had indicated she merely had a superficial infection.[29]

Even with all the best evidence in the world's top hospitals, medicine remains "an imperfect science, an enterprise of constantly changing knowledge, uncertain information, fallible individuals, and at the same time lives on the line. There is science in what we do, yes, but also habit, intuition, and sometimes plain old guessing."[30] In Gawande's case examples, the evidence of objective tests gave way to years of painstakingly acquired professional experience that helped doctors make quick decisions that saved people's lives.

Gawande advanced a complicated argument with profound implications for schools in his second book, *Better*.[31] Every year, he notes, 2 million Americans acquire additional infections in hospitals. Of these, an astonishing 90,000 die. Eradicating hospital infections, however, requires more than collecting data and confronting people with it.

If they followed the strict guidelines established by the U.S. Centers for Disease Control, staff would spend a third of their workday just washing their hands. Doctors and nurses have to decide not just whether to wash their hands, but whether to wash their hands or rush to attend to a gunshot wound that won't stop bleeding, or whether to wash their hands or assist an elderly patient who has suddenly collapsed.

All kinds of top-down mandates and prescriptions were used to respond to these disturbing dilemmas—having staff carry purifying gels with them, taking nasal cultures of all incoming patients to check for infections, and relocating supplies to save time when acquiring them. These reforms either had no impact or lost their impact when the supervisor who implemented them switched jobs.

A breakthrough solution to all of these troubling dilemmas related to the spread of infections finally came when Jon Lloyd, a surgeon in Pittsburgh, decided to try cultural change through "positive deviance," building on the skills and knowledge staff already had rather than mandating how to change.[32] Thirty-minute small-group discussions with staff at all levels brought forth a cornucopia of ideas about how to address the problem. Nurses plucked up courage to tell doctors to wash their hands. Staff began wearing gloves. Progress was communicated on a monthly basis. In just one year, deaths from infections plunged to zero.

Following Gawande's line of reasoning, we do need data. Data alert us to disturbing realities that can and must be confronted. Tracking data can tell us when we're making progress and when we need to adjust. But institutional realities are messy. This is when statistical data have to be combined with professional judgment in a culture of shared learning and insight in which all staff, from cafeteria workers to top administrators, contribute to solving a problem. When Lloyd asked staff for their ideas, "Many . . . said it was the first time anyone had ever asked them what to do."[33]

This combination of evidence and experience in communities of practice and committed problem solving is what we all need. But before we spell out the implications more fully, let's turn from the life and death world of hospitals to the win/lose realities of sport.

Michael Lewis has written a best-selling book, *Moneyball: The Art of Winning an Unfair Game*, about the outstanding success of the Oakland Athletics baseball team.[34] His story is extraordinary because this success was achieved *after* the team's biggest financial backers had pulled out, leaving Oakland wondering whether the franchise could survive. The question Lewis asks is " How did the second poorest team in baseball . . . stand even the faintest chance of success, much less the ability to win more regular season games than all but one of the other twenty-nine teams?"[35]

The answer is that Oakland became the first baseball franchise to take baseball fans' fascination with players' statistics seriously as a basis for their recruitment strategy. Before the arrival of new general manager Billy Beane in 2002, baseball coaches scoured the country, looking for high school talent, relying on their experience and intuition to find young men who had "a body that looked as if it had been created to wear a baseball uniform."[36] Armed with only a laptop and a sidekick computer nerd with a BA in economics from Harvard, Beane took a risk and opted instead for "performance scouting" based on what college students had already done—*not* what they might become.[37]

Beane bucked scouting lore and traditions to recruit players with strong performance records documented in hard data—not prima donnas with the right build or connections. He most favored the statistic that best predicts the performance of a team over a season: on-base percentage (the proportion of times a batter is able to reach first base without getting out). The most dramatic way to do this is with power hitting—a line drive over the head of the shortstop or a double off the center field wall. Not surprisingly, that's what the coaches, and many of the fans, like the most.

But there are other ways to get to first base, most of them quite wimpy. For example, you can bunt the ball—giving it a devious little tap into an area and at a time the fielders least expect it—and then run! Or you can draw a walk to first base by having a good sense of your strike zone (the area over the plate that you have to defend—like an imaginary wicket in cricket) and not striking at a pitch outside the zone! Or if you are overweight or fidget over the plate to irritate the pitcher as he starts his wind-up, you can get hit by a pitch, giving you a free trip to first! Big hitters don't always yield the best stats.

The details matter less than the overall theory-in-action. First, recognize the overriding importance of the on-base statistic. Second, select players who fit it even though they come in strange shapes and sizes and *don't look at all* as if they were born to wear a uniform. Third, train the players to focus on getting on base as a routine process.

Oakland played the percentages with remarkable results. More players made it to first base, which was one step closer to home plate and scoring. Year after year, lowly Oakland made it to the play-offs, where they faced teams earning triple their payroll. In the Oakland A's, cumulative evidence defied individual experience, intuition, and habit.

But, once more, there is an equally persuasive but contrary argument. Sports leaders, like medical doctors, can rely too much on the statistics and neglect the human side of their organizations. One of us has been studying organizations that perform above expectations, including professional sport teams.[38] With fellow researcher Alan Boyle, we interviewed a wiry young man in the backroom of an English Championship League soccer team. His job title was "Performance Analyst." The major tool at his disposal was something called "ProZone." ProZone is not the new performance drug of choice for soccer players! Rather, it is a computer program that tracks individual player performances through analysis of game videos culled from a number of static cameras placed around the soccer field.

After every game, the film tapes go outside the club for raw analysis, then come back to the Performance Analyst, who compiles an analysis for each player. The data are exhaustive. "Every touch of the ball—where they are, when they touched it, what they did afterwards.... There's nothing that's missed." Amounts, kinds, and quality of passing; parts of the field covered; amount of running and energy expenditure—all these things are calculated. So how do players use the data to improve their performance on the field?

Some managers, we were told, treat the data literally, as an unambiguous indicator of effort and effectiveness. A few had even placed microchips in their players' footwear to gather data about the number of steps they took during a game. The Performance Analyst, who had studied the program for his Masters of Science, commented:

> In the World Cup...they tried out that technology and I believe there were some players who started doing extra steps when the ball went out of play (out of sight of the cameras) so they could up their stats—tell the manager—"yes, I've done my job this week." There's always ways around it![39]

Contrary to this autocratic imposition of step requirements, the club we studied, like the hospital unit in Pittsburgh, developed a more interactive and inclusive approach to evidence. This included sharing data with the manager; suggesting what it meant in terms of performance or energy levels; inviting players to look at their statistics and see how they compared to average performance levels in the league—and then discussing specific ways to improve together. "The data *contributes* rather than *dictating* what they should do," the Performance Analyst commented. "Whether it is technical or tactical, you can have a different interpretation of it." Responding to the data with commands would be sure to fail, because to "prescribe what to do" would "take away the spontaneity and creativity" that accords with the club's philosophy of "freedom of expression"[40]:

> My strength is to find that information and bring it to [the managers'] attention and then from that they can make their decisions. It's a relationship like you wouldn't want to start telling people what to do. And the same with the players as well. I want to help them improve, I want to help them play their best, but it's approaching it in the right way so as not to annoy people or tread on any toes.[41]

This sports club uses data intelligently, invitationally, and inclusively. It doesn't treat statistical evidence as gospel truth leading to unarguable commandments, but rather as a process of interaction in a professional learning community where everyone wants to improve. Players on this professional team see data as their companion—not as their commander.

Teachers, like sports clubs, can overvalue their intuition. Like the coaches who choose players who remind them of themselves, teachers also can fall foul by using practical judgment alone. We know this because we have been among the perpetrators. For years, we confess, we didn't really like student performance rubrics—or level descriptions, as they are known in England. While we agreed it was good to have clear criteria for assessment, rubrics just seemed to go too far. How could the entire world, almost, be divided into four levels of proficiency? After decades of marriage, perhaps we would still be "emerging" as husbands! We criticized this obsession with rubrics. It was turning into a plague of "rubricosis," we said.

But then, we thought, perhaps we should try this ourselves before dismissing it. So we set out to produce the best rubric we could to assess the written assignments of our graduate students. And we learned something important about ourselves: We love writing. We like the style, the music, and the poetry of it. And our students know this. However, our rubrics taught us, we loved writing too much, so much so that we had been giving less credit to students who could write clearly but not elegantly, who had great ideas but couldn't express them perfectly, who applied evidence well but not always in the most compelling way. We had been rewarding students who reminded us of ourselves! We needed the data to draw us away from ourselves and back to the students. And so do all teachers, especially when our students are not altogether like us in their culture, or in the ways they learn or show their learning best.

This acknowledgment of the benefits of data when they are carefully adapted by individual teachers who work as skilled artisans, however, has turned into yet another excuse for mandates and prescriptions. Too often, schools and school systems use data and research evidence much less intelligently and flexibly than this. For instance, they

- dictate that every teacher present a three-part lesson. *How would this work with art or drama?*
- require that learning targets and lesson objectives always be posted on the board for students to see. *But what about the lessons that creative teachers cherish, which contain an element of surprise that keeps students on their toes, or even lessons where students determine their own learning objectives?*
- insist that all parents read to their children at bedtime. *But most Chinese parents, for instance, don't have this tradition but develop literacy in their children in other ways.*
- prescribe and pace a "scientifically proven" way of teaching literacy that was documented in a number of carefully controlled experiments with selected populations. *This would be like treating patients in one messy, real-world setting by rigidly following practices that worked in an altogether untypical laboratory context.*
- give elementary teachers smaller classes rather than a paid classroom assistant. *We will see in Chapter 3 that this research finding only holds for controlled experiments in snapshots of time, not in the longer-term real life of school.*
- prioritize increased state test scores above everything else. *This is true even when the resulting test preparation leads to declines in the more sophisticated performances and achievements required by college entrance examinations.*

Other schools and school systems, however, use data more mindfully in communities of inquiry and action where evidence and experience inform each other through a continuous cycle of data analysis, reflection, action, and assessment. Amanda Datnow and her colleagues, for example, found that high-achieving elementary and secondary schools defined data in a broad way, including minutes of faculty meetings and narrative observations of colleagues' teaching.[42] They combined multiple data sources, engaged students in discussions of what the assessment data conveyed, and used these deliberations as a point of departure for larger investigations of teaching, learning, and school culture.

Educational performance data deserve intelligent interpretation. Indeed, sustainable improvement depends on it. When statistical data provide one source of information among many, when educators approach the data in a spirit of curiosity and inquiry rather than in a climate of panic and fear, and when teachers have the professional discretion to use data to justify trying innovative approaches without anxiety and intimidation, then data can play a powerful role in improving learning and increasing achievement. But data that are misleading or misinterpreted only distract us from this purpose—as do data that are misused.

3. MISUSED DATA

Perhaps the most disturbing characteristic of technocracies is how the top-down use of high-stakes performance data can slant the system towards trickery and treachery. In business, this is exactly what happened with Enron, when the constant pressure for improvement in quarterly returns led to creative accountancy and, ultimately, to fraud. We have seen in soccer's ProZone how excessive oversight of players can lead them to take lots of extra steps that are utterly unnecessary—just to keep the manager off their backs. When data are used to drive and deliver reform according to an unarguable and imposed political agenda, teachers and schools also quickly learn to take unnecessary extra steps. This is "gaming the system"—manipulating and maneuvering around it in order to survive—and we have seen a lot of it in the Second Way, and indeed in the Third Way, as well.

Too many teachers today are constrained to concentrate on tested literacy and mathematics—marginalizing other areas of the curriculum such as social studies, the environment, or the arts. Demanding that schools be data driven leads many of them to concentrate only on the tests in cultures of anxiety about instant results. Those in poorer communities, especially, find themselves on a data-driven treadmill, poised on a precipice of failure and unwanted intervention.

Especially in the overtested environment of America, where the Second Way of standardization still prevails at the time of this book's release, professional learning communities are turning school staffrooms into a "turnstile world" of transient teamwork where mathematicians, statisticians, and soulless technocrats have taken over the educational academy.[43] As Betty Achinstein and Rodney Ogawa reported in the *Harvard Educational Review*, when teachers—even instructionally superb teachers—question these regimes of pedagogical prescription and improvement-by-numbers, they can find themselves vilified as "independent contractors" rather than "team players."[44] In the worst cases, they are banished from their schools and districts without so much as a reference.

- In Ontario, one of the eight schools in the *Change Over Time* study responded to a newly imposed 10th-grade literacy test by pretesting the students and getting the English Department to concentrate its test preparation on the 20% of students just below the passing mark—to the neglect of the other 80% of students.
- In New York, a magnet school in the same study prospered by promoting standards-based reform among its high-achieving students, but consigned the special education students it was required to accommodate to the school's basement. When some of the school's teachers protested, they found themselves banished to the basement, too.[45]
- A primary school in London was among the worst in the country in the late 1990s and achieved a miraculous turnaround that eventually propelled it to the level of the national average 10 years later. Yet, the school initially attained this result by questionable means. They assigned the few stronger teachers to Year 6 (the Key Stage 2 testing point), drilling those teachers in test preparation procedures, and obliging them to abandon all other areas of the curriculum except the areas that were being tested. Because there was great improvement in Year 6 but none in Year 2 (Key Stage 1) where the weaker teachers remained, the school was able to register a phenomenal record in demonstrating value-added student progress between the two key stages, and so came to be counted among the most improved schools in the nation.[46]

In these Second Way situations, the technocratic distractions were blindingly obvious. They led to cynical, quick-fix strategies to appease administrative superiors and create the appearances of improvement that would keep politicians and the public at bay.

In the Third Way, though, the technocratic distractions have become more subtle and diffuse. Teachers are no longer disciplined if they perform badly. Data are now used to get teachers to monitor and discipline *themselves* through sophisticated systems of self-surveillance.

In the New Orthodoxy, schools don't just react to testing, targets, and Adequate Yearly Progress. Instead, they anticipate and prepare for them—with a vengeance. Every reading program, curriculum choice, professional development workshop, and teaching strategy is scrutinized and selected in order to meet the targets. Whatever is in the autocratic system leader's mind, it seems, should already be in every classroom in the nation, through educators' unquestioning compliance with the omnipotent and omnipresent data.

In these systems of surveillance, instead of being informed intelligently by evidence in cultures of trusted relationships that deepen and develop learning and achievement, professional learning communities of teachers turn into add-on teams of thrown-together staff who are driven by data in cultures of instant results. Data-driven decision making ends up driving teachers to distraction—away from the passionate enthusiasm for rich processes of teaching and learning in classrooms and into the target-centered tunnel vision of the technocrat.[47] More test preparation here, more after-school classes there, more concentration on cells of children who fall just below the failure line elsewhere—all this anticipates the pressures of a system that believes data can enable it to know when and where to intervene with any student, school, or classroom, at any time. Precision has turned into an obsession.

In the New Orthodoxy, these cultures of data-driven improvement aren't always unwanted or oppressive. Gaming the system—and savoring the public rewards for doing so—can be enjoyable and exhilarating. Carefully coached by their teachers, and assisted by data that identify weak points where they need to adjust their instruction, teachers provide students with the calculated assistance that ensures their test scores go up. The results can be uplifting. Teachers weep tears of joy when principals read test results over the intercom or when superintendents announce student achievement gains. Students enjoy cake and ice cream at effusive victory celebrations. Real estate agents place newspaper articles about improved scores in glossy packages advertising the high quality of life in residential neighborhoods. This is when educators find themselves on a third distracting path—the *Path of Effervescence*.

THE PATH OF EFFERVESCENCE

The distractions of the Path of Effervescence are appealing and entertaining. In a carnival of collegiality, this path solves the motivation deficits created by top-down standardization and market-based reforms by stimulating and spreading increased professional engagement and interaction. Teachers interact with teachers, schools learn from schools, and the strong help the weak. This is not only an empowering and effective way to approach improvement, but it's also lots of fun. Of course, fun is not the same as happiness. Real happiness is found through taking on worthy challenges, often against formidable odds, that address our purposes—challenges that we ourselves have played a role in choosing. Fun is merely the fleeting pleasure of an evanescent "high."

In the New Orthodoxy, increased lateral interaction among teachers and schools often amounts to a kind of hyperactive professionalism. Educators rush around, energetically and enthusiastically delivering the government's narrowly defined targets and purposes, rather than also developing and realizing inspiring purposes of their own. Schools become addictive organizations, obsessed with meeting targets, raising performance standards, and adjusting strategies right down to intervening with every individual child.[48] One leader in the *Raising Achievement, Transforming Learning (RATL)* project of underperforming schools spoke enthusiastically of how the school could get "exposure to good practice in other places that we can bring back here . . . and customize if we think that it's a good strategy for our school."[49] Each jump in scores gives educators another fix to exchange and apply more of the same short-term strategies, focused on measurable results. Success is celebrated in morale-boosting ceremonies and emotionally uplifting announcements. There may be heightened performance on tests, but is the teaching and learning really better? And what kinds of cultures are we creating in our schools in the process? Let's turn to our own research evidence again:

- In Texas schools, educators held "Texas Assessment of Academic Skills (TAAS) pep rallies" and "school lockdowns" to get ready for the state's standardized tests. Teachers wrote poems about their students excelling on the tests and read them out in packed gymnasiums.[50]
- In Boston, a first-year teacher was asked by his cheery assistant principal when he wanted to do "Massachusetts Comprehensive Assessment System (MCAS) camp" (a euphemism for test-preparatory classes)—before school, after school, or on Saturdays?[51]
- In England, a promising improvement network of underperforming schools (which we will describe in the Chapter 3) hurriedly and excitedly swapped successful strategies with their mentors and each other on their meetings and school visits.[52] Yet the overwhelming majority of strategies that teachers adopted were simple and short-term strategies, such as paying former students to mentor current students, having examiners share their grading schemes with students, establishing ways for students to access study strategies online from peers in other schools, bringing in motivational speakers for at-risk groups like minority boys, and supplying bananas and water to hydrate the brain and raise potassium levels on test days. Educators were excited about these strategies. They thought they were "gimmicky and great" and were hungry for more when they saw the impact on tested student achievement. But they sidelined the more challenging and mindful professional conversations about transforming their teaching and learning practices that the networks' directors wanted to achieve.

The idea of increased and improved professional interaction is admirable. Teachers have been starved for it for too long. But the Third

Way's promise of lateral engagement of the profession and the public has become diluted by top-down controls that restrict what all this interaction can achieve.

Instead, much of it amounts to a kind of "collective effervescence" of light and bubbly energy. French sociologist Émile Durkheim first used this term to describe how people have to experience intense emotion from time to time if they are truly to feel like members of a community.[53] Stjepan Meštrović tells us that it's exactly when we are most harried and constrained in today's fast and flexible society that we are provided with and respond to short bursts of technologically simulated emotion.[54] Advertisements for cars and cell phones offer passion and desire. Schools get high on professional effervescence when test scores go up. Graduation award ceremonies spread to every grade level, celebrating what was once taken for granted as a routine step in development. Teacher of the Year Awards offer public moments of emotional catharsis, with outstanding teachers celebrated for their creativity and the passion they infuse into their classrooms, even as they and their colleagues swim upstream to avoid drowning in a torrent of technical data.

All this effervescence is distractingly fun and easy compared with building and committing to deeper relations of trust in long-term communities that take the time to pursue and achieve inspiring and challenging goals that benefit students together. As with Lewis Carroll's Cheshire cat from *Alice in Wonderland*, perhaps we should worry when the smile of professional interaction lingers long after the body has disappeared. We do indeed need more collegial interaction, lateral learning, and professional fulfillment in school reform. But these reforms must be substantial and profound, not data driven and contrived.

CONCLUSION

The original Third Way held out great promise. It offered balance instead of polarization. It proposed ways to help people so they could help themselves—corresponding to the Iron Rule of community organizing that one *never, ever should do for others what they can do for themselves.* It advocated more professional freedom, but not without responsibility. It restored respect for educators and increased public investment in their work. Even the most disillusioned critics of how the Third Way has turned out would never want to go back to the mean-spirited politics of the Second Way or the inconsistency and sporadic self-indulgence of the First. But, in education, the Third Way has been driven off course by three distracters that are now embedded in a powerful New Orthodoxy of autocracy, technocracy, and effervescence. The relationship of this Third Way to its predecessors is represented in Figure 2.1.

We are at a critical turning point. More free-market competition or autocratic imposition are not the answers. Data must be our servant, not our savior—still less our omnipotent and omnipresent superior. And increased professional interaction should not just inject educators with quick motivational lifts that produce short-term improvements in superficial results, but also must engage teachers together and with others in transforming the very purposes and processes of teaching and learning for the 21st century.

Figure 2.1   From the First Way to the Third Way of Educational Change

	The First Way	The Interregnum	The Second Way	The Third Way
Control	Professionalism	Professionalism and bureaucracy	Bureaucracy and markets	Bureaucracy, markets, and professionalism
Purpose	Innovation and inspiration	Quest for coherence	Markets and standardization	Performance and partnership
Trust	Passive trust	Growing suspicion	Active mistrust	Public confidence
Community engagement	Mainly absent	Parent communication	Parent choice	Delivery of services to communities
Curriculum	Inconsistent innovation	Broad standards and outcomes	Detailed and prescribed standardization	Varying prescription with increased coaching and support
Teaching and learning	Eclectic and uneven	Prescriptively driven by standards and testing	Direct instruction to standards and test requirements	Autocratically data driven yet customized
Professionalism	Autonomous	Increasingly collaborative	Deprofessionalized	Reprofessionalized
Professional learning communities	Discretionary	Some collaborative cultures	Contrived collegiality	Data driven and professionally effervescent
Assessment and accountability	Local and sampled	Portfolio and performance-based	High-stakes targets and testing by census	Escalating targets, self-surveillance, and testing-by-census
Lateral relations	Voluntary	Consultative	Competitive	Networked

The three paths of distraction all lead to the same place: a culture of addictive presentism in which swift solutions and instant highs give an effervescent lift to hurried professionals. They help politicians meet the short-term targets that get them through the next election and keep them in office. Do as we say! Do it quickly! Do it now! Think not of the past that has shaped you, nor the sustainable future we should leave to those who follow. Think only of engaging in immediate interactions and responding to the overwhelming pressures of data and demands, right here, right now!

In the opening lines of this chapter, John Ralston Saul, Canadian philosopher, essayist, and novelist, admonishes those managers whose self-interest leads them to drown people in the short term. George Orwell famously warned us that the person "who controls the past, controls the future; who controls the present controls the past."[55] The three paths of distraction erase a collectively imagined future and a shared and defining past by ensuring people live only in and for the present.

The New Orthodoxy is busy, *but it isn't always better.* As the Third Way has evolved, it has not put the passion back into teaching nor the pleasure into learning. In societies of increasing cultural diversity, we need more and not fewer ways to connect the classroom to children's lives. Economic competitiveness cries out for more creativity, but we remain boxed into the basics. When our planet is ecologically imperiled and too much of our world is unsafe, we need to help children not just raise their test scores, but also to want to build a better future and have the knowledge, skills, and dispositions to do so. The elephant in the room of the Third Way has been an excess of government control. It is now time to forge a Fourth Way that will create more room inside the government elephant.

It's time for a change that is disruptive, not incremental.[56] It's time to bring the magic and wonder back into teaching. It's time to recover the missionary spirit and deep moral purpose of engaging and inspiring all our students. It's time to put down the spreadsheets and look to each other and elsewhere for how to get beyond the present turning point so we can transform our society and our schools. It's time to stop "belting out loud notes" and to show our true strength by learning to "let go" a little. The worst of the Old Ways must now be set aside as we find and forge a New Way ahead.

———— ■■ ————

*I lift up mine eyes unto the hills, from whence
cometh my help.*

——PSALMS 121:1

CHAPTER THREE

THE FOUR HORIZONS OF HOPE

The Top-Performing Nation

The Innovative and Effective Network

The Democratic Movement

The Turned-Around District

E ach Way of change has left a legacy—a mixture of strengths and weaknesses, good and bad. The philosopher George Santayana warned that if we do not learn from the past, we are condemned to repeat it.[1] History is not a pile of refuse, nor is it a refuge. Our challenge, in relation to our values and our vision, is to learn from history what we can and to leave behind what we must. What, in this sense, have the first three ways of change bequeathed to us?

- Retrieving the spirit of innovation and flexibility of the First Way can restore the capacity of teachers to create much of their own curriculum and rekindle the inspiration of world-changing social and educational missions that bind teachers together and connect them to ideals beyond themselves.
- From the interregnum, we can take the guiding power of broadly defined common standards, the importance of personally supporting each student, and the technical advances of portfolio and performance assessments that began to make complex and authentic assessments part of the learning process, and not just judgments about learning that was already over.

- The Second Way of standardization bequeathed a sense of urgency about educational inequities and drew attention to the underperformance and the needs of *all* students in every school—not just the high achievers or those who keep the school's performance average up. The Second Way improved the quality of some skill-specific training, coaching, and teaching and gave unprecedented prominence to achievement data as an instrument to challenge the negative stereotypes that teachers sometimes hold about the abilities of students from poor and minority families.

- The Third Way ameliorated the discourse of disgrace that had humiliated struggling schools and teachers, made education a high priority for policymakers of all stripes, and increased the resources and support allocated to public education. Because of the Third Way, the teaching profession is recovering public respect and enjoying increased involvement with colleagues as agents of improvement, and not just as objects of reform. Moreover, the database of comparative performance among schools, departments, or teachers no longer operates as a blunt instrument of crude test rankings that ignore the contexts in which people work. Instead, that database now provides a sophisticated and well-stocked chest of precision tools that can enhance real improvement.

The contrasts and overlaps between these different ways of change are represented in Figure 3.1.

Figure 3.1   What to Retain and What to Abandon

	... Retain	... Abandon
First Way	Inspiration, innovation, and autonomy	Inconsistency and professional license
Interregnum	Common standards with local interpretation	Weak development of teachers, leaders, and communities
Second Way	Urgency, consistency, and all-inclusive equity	Cut-throat competition and excessive standardization
Third Way	Balance and inclusiveness, public involvement, financial reinvestment, better evidence, and professional networks	Persistent autocracy, imposed targets, obsession with data, effervescent interactions

The lessons of almost four decades of educational change show us what we should *abandon* as much as what we should *retain*. How do we return to the innovation and creativity of the 1960s and early 1970s, yet avoid unacceptable inconsistencies in professional competence and quality? How do we preserve and promote the commitment to high standards that marked the reforms of the 1980s, while evading the dead hand of standardization? How can we retain the rightful sense of urgency about immediate improvement of the 1990s without perpetuating target-driven tyranny? Can we keep the upbeat lateral energy and activity of professional networks that have emerged in the Third Way, while ensuring they have solidity and substance as well as zest and zing? And how can those at the top exercise their responsibilities to set and secure reform directions without turning into micromanagers and control freaks?

OUTLIERS OF INNOVATION AND IMPROVEMENT

In recent years, we have found ourselves moving beyond what some critics call "misery research" on all that is wrong with schools and school systems towards an appreciative inquiry into what seems to be working well.[2] People who work in successful systems are usually proud of their results but often baffled about what explains them. But if a succinct way can be found to explain what a system does well, it is easier for others to learn to apply the core principles behind it in their own way. In this sense, we can avoid transplanting isolated elements—such as Finnish teachers' master's degrees or high numbers of annual instructional hours in Japan—as simple solutions for educational success.[3]

This keystone chapter points to four horizons of hope that suggest ways forward as we carve a route out of the entanglements of ineffective change in which we have become trapped: (1) a whole country, (2) a large network of schools, (3) community organizing, and (4) a school district.

Horizons draw our eyes towards the distance. They define the very edge of our existing vision. Spread all around the compass, they provide points of focus to possible ways forward. Horizons are not destinations. They provide landmarks on a journey that offer their own viewpoints and that can (but do not always) motivate travelers to find and forge their paths ahead. As German philosopher Hans-Georg Gadamer advised us, "Applying this to the thinking mind, we speak of narrowness of horizon, of the possible expansion of horizon, of the opening up of new horizons, and so forth."[4] Horizons are our future starting points. They are, at their best, our geography of hope.

The four horizons in this chapter are not individual schools. As long as schools have existed, exceptional schools under charismatic leaders have always stood out from the crowd, but the achievements of these schools typically fade over time. Either the exceptions become less exceptional, or they remain as marginal outsiders that do not affect the mainstream of educational life. Tangible hope, rather, must be evident in entire systems—in whole collections of schools—that reveal how profound change can benefit the many, and can continue to do so across different leaders and over many years.

The first horizon of hope is *a whole country*—small in population compared with some, but similar in size to many of the states and provinces that are the prime units of systemic change in various nations. This country ranks highest in the world on many measures of educational achievement and on many social and economic indicators. If we want to learn how to improve, it's best to learn not from those who are behind us or who perform as poorly as we do, but from people and systems that are ahead— including the very best in the world.

The second horizon is *a large network of schools* that brought about significant achievement gains in a relatively short period. More and more systems are turning to professional networks of teachers, leaders, and schools to energize and orchestrate improvement. Big, bumbling bureaucracies or isolated and inward-looking districts are coming to be seen as change obstacles rather than improvement assets. In contrast, networks offer a flexible and professionally motivating mechanism of improvement within and beyond districts. Teachers learn from talking to other teachers and exchanging strategies that seem to work. Not all networks succeed, however. Learning from high-performing networks can pinpoint what kinds of network architecture and activities work best.

The third horizon of hope is that of *community organizing* as a positive force for educational change. Some of the most effective educational change efforts do not begin directly with governments, although governments can create the conditions in which they flourish. These reform movements work *around* government, *beside* it, and sometimes even *against* it. We define community organizing broadly here—as forms of civic and public engagement that originate in neighborhoods, faith-based institutions, labor unions, local businesses, and philanthropic foundations.

The fourth and last horizon is *a school district* serving a large immigrant population that overcame years of low expectations and official neglect to rise from the bottom of the national league tables to the middle of the pack in just under a decade. This case indicates that when leadership is strong, when the community is engaged, when schools and educators work together, and when the government provides additional resources for change, extraordinary and sustainable success can be achieved even within national contexts that are still dominated by the New Orthodoxy of data-driven targets and testing.

Whether you are learning from a country or a state, or from a network, community, or district, it's important to approach this learning in the right spirit. Just as it is not possible to replicate a Stradivarius violin, or completely emulate an outstanding tennis professional or expert teacher, it is not feasible to import change off the shelf, either. There are three reasons for this:

1. You can't just adopt the end product of something that took others years to develop. It's the slowly built understanding of the development that makes much of the implementation effective. This was evident when the outstanding literacy reform strategy that had taken 10 years to develop in New York District 2 was transported unsuccessfully to San Diego within an implementation timeline of just two years. This was far too short and rushed a period for deep understandings of literacy to develop and flourish as they had in New York.[5]

2. No two places are alike. Novice teachers can learn a lot by watching highly experienced colleagues, but they can rarely copy them completely because their styles and personalities as well as accompanying skill sets are just too different. For the same reason, countries cannot be cloned either. Each has a distinctive "personality" in the form of its cultures and histories.

3. The Greek philosopher Heraclitus famously said, "No man ever steps in the same river twice, for it is not the same river and he is not the same man." In the same vein, countries, networks, districts, and particular instances of community organizing strategies cannot be replicated. Nevertheless, they can be cross-pollinated with other successful reform initiatives and movements—including our own.

THE TOP-PERFORMING NATION

In 2007, one of us served with a team from the Organization for Economic Cooperation and Development (OECD) that included Gábor Halász and Beatriz Pont to investigate and report on the relationship between leadership and school improvement in Finland.[6] This nation in northern Europe is the world's number 1 or 2 performer for children at age 15 in literacy, mathematics, and science, according to the influential OECD Programme for International Student Assessment (PISA) tables. Finland is also high in economic competitiveness and corporate transparency. In addition, Martti Ahtisaari, Finland's president during the vital growth years of 1994–2000, was awarded the Nobel Peace Prize in 2008.

We visited schools and districts and interviewed students, teachers, principals, system administrators, university researchers, and senior ministry officials about their society and their system. A remarkably unified narrative began to surface about the country, its schools, and their sense of aspiration, struggle, and destiny. Finland has endured centuries of dependency on and oppression by its Swedish and Russian neighbors and only achieved true independence in 1917. In the context of this historical legacy, and in the face of a harsh climate and northern geography, it is not surprising that one of the most popular Finnish sayings translates as, "It was long and it was hard, but we did it!"

Yet it is not simply stoic perseverance, fed by a Lutheran religious ethic of hard work and resilience, that explains Finland's enviable status as a high-performing educational system and economy. At the core of Finland's success and sustainability is its capacity to reconcile, harmonize, and integrate a high-performing economy, a superb school system, and a socially just society. Contrast this with the Anglo-American countries, where material wealth has been gained at the expense of increasing social division, and at the expense of children's well-being. The United Kingdom and the United States ranked dead last and next to last, respectively, on the UNICEF 2007 international survey of child well-being. Finland, by comparison, ranked fourth.[7]

Finland's record of economic and educational success is relatively recent. In the 1950s, it was a rural backwater; at the end of the 1990s when the end of the Cold War had closed down Finland's captive Soviet market, unemployment spiralled up to 19%. Finland knew that to survive in the new economy it would have to learn how to respond to external change more swiftly and effectively than did competing nations. It therefore set about designing a creative, high-skill, high-wage knowledge economy in which people invent, apply, share, and circulate knowledge at a level that surpasses all competitors.

The Nokia telecommunications company, whose operations and suppliers account for about 40% of the country's gross domestic product (GDP), exemplifies Finnish knowledge society attributes. Its flexible workplace organization requires management to change jobs every 15 months to enhance organizational learning and accelerate communication about difficulties or shortcomings throughout the company. At Nokia, they say, bad news must travel fast.[8]

Educational reform has been central to Finland's transformation from the economic crisis of the early 1990s to a high-tech powerhouse of the 21st century. One key reform has been the decentralization of the educational system to increase creativity and flexibility, yet this is within an inspiring and commonly held social vision that connects a creative and prosperous future to the Finn's sense of themselves as having a common social identity and creative, craft-like past.

Science and technology are top Finnish priorities in fuelling economic competitiveness. Almost 3% of GDP is allocated to scientific and technological development. A national committee that includes leading corporate executives and university presidents, chaired by the prime minister, steers and integrates economic and educational strategy. Yet technological creativity and competitiveness do not break Finns from their past, but connect them to it in a compelling and inspiring narrative of lifelong learning and social development. In tune with their artistic and creative identity, all young people engage in creative, visual, and performing arts until the end of secondary school, with musical instruments paid for by the state. In Finland, there are more symphony orchestra conductors per capita than in any other country.

All this occurs in a strong welfare state that supports the educational system and the economy. Public education provides schooling free of charge as a universal and constitutional right, from well-funded early childhood education all the way through higher education. Students receive all necessary resources and free school meals regardless of their social class, so the middle classes participate in, benefit from, and support the welfare state.

Finnish analysts have remarked that all this educational and economic integration occurs in a society that values educators as servants of the public good and creators of the country's future. This enables Finland to attract high-quality teachers, who all possess graduate degrees. Although teachers are paid only at the OECD average, high school graduates rank teaching as their most desired occupation. Because of the social mission and resulting status of teaching, Finns are able to make entry into the profession highly competitive, with applicants to primary teacher education programs having less than a 10% chance of acceptance.

In Finland, the state *steers* but does not *prescribe* in detail the national curriculum. Trusted teams of highly qualified teachers write much of the curriculum at the level of the municipality, in ways that adjust to the students they know best. In schools characterized by an uncanny calmness, teachers say they feel responsible for all children in their school—not just those in their own classes, subjects, or grade levels. And they collaborate quietly on all their students' behalf in cultures of trust, cooperation, and responsibility.

Finns told us they perform well not because they create geniuses, but because they lift up every individual child from the bottom at the first signs of difficulty. Teachers work with small classes of normally no more than 24 students. They are not distracted by having to respond to endless initiatives and targeted interventions. This enables them to know their children well. Individual classroom assistants are available in most schools to help teachers who have students with special needs. Special education is based on early prevention rather than repair and is offered full- or part- time, depending on individual needs. School well-being teams including teachers, administrators, welfare workers, and the school nurse meet regularly to discuss and support all children in danger of falling behind.

School principals in Finland are required by law to have been teachers themselves (no business or military transplants here!). Most continue to be engaged in classroom teaching for at least two hours per week. This gives them credibility among their teachers, enables them to stay connected to the students, and helps ensure that leadership for learning is not merely high-flown rhetoric, but rather a living reality.

How is it, principals were asked, that they could not only lead their schools, but also find the time to teach? "Because," one said, "unlike the Anglo-Saxon countries, we do not have to spend our time responding to long, long lists of government initiatives that come from the top." Interestingly, Finland has no system of standardized testing except for confidential samples for monitoring purposes. There is no indigenous Finnish term for *accountability*. Instead, public education is seen as a collective social and professional *responsibility*. In direct opposition to the New Orthodoxy, Finland achieves high performance without constantly taking public measures of it.

Teachers and principals view the principal's role as being one of a "society of experts" whose task is to draw knowledge and ideas *out* of colleagues rather than driving initiatives *through* them. Indeed, if the principal should fall sick or have a prolonged absence for any reason, teachers say they simply take over the school because it belongs to all of them.

In the city of Tampere, many principals have taken on significant responsibilities across the municipality as well as within their own schools, prompting them to develop and distribute greater leadership capacity within their schools while they are working systemwide. More than this, the principals recognized they are not just responsible for children in their own schools, but rather are jointly responsible for all the children of Tampere— for the future of the city and the civic pride they invest in it. If resources are lacking for a needed initiative, a principal contacts colleagues who respond, "We have a little bit extra—would you like some of ours?"

Finland is not a typical country or a perfect one. It is culturally homogeneous compared with Anglo-American nations, although this has changed since the country became a member of the European Union in 1995. It has one of the widest gaps among OECD nations between male and female student achievement. As more and more children look less and less like their teachers, empathy for students' struggles and difficulties may require more than teachers exercising their intuitive judgment alone. Additional assessment instruments may need to be employed to add to their intuition. In addition, Finland's welfare state is struggling to stay sustainable as the aging Baby Boomer generation drives up already high taxes because of its retirement requirements, and public funding is not as abundant as it was.

Nonetheless, Finland contains essential lessons for knowledge societies that seek to educate students beyond the narrow and constraining skill sets of the New Orthodoxy. The lessons are these:

- Build an inspiring and inclusive future by wedding it to the past.
- Foster strong connections between education and economic development through scientific and technological innovation, without sacrificing culture and creativity.
- Raise standards by lifting the many, rather than by pushing a privileged few.
- Support inclusive special education through prevention more than repair.
- Control teacher quality at the point of entry by affirming a mission that attracts the very best candidates, then providing rigorous training through university-based, school-connected programs.
- Commit to collegial cultures of trust, cooperation, and responsibility.
- Develop more curriculum that is locally and culturally responsive.
- Share responsibility for all children's futures across a town or a city, not just those in your own schools or classes.
- Steer the educational system governmentally, but don't micromanage or interfere in the details of it.

These are just some of the signs about possible reform pathways that we can take from Finland's exceptional educational and economic achievements.

THE INNOVATIVE AND EFFECTIVE NETWORK

In 2005, we were approached by the U.K. Specialist Schools and Academies Trust (which now coordinates more than 90% of secondary schools and academies in England) to study and report on a school improvement network it had established. Our mandate was simple and direct: Could we make explicit the model behind the project's success that was implicit and unclear at the time?

The project was entitled *Raising Achievement, Transforming Learning (RATL)*.[9] It included more than 300 secondary schools that had experienced a dip in student achievement scores over one or two years. This was a large network with a distinctive change model funded from public and private resources. It promoted improvement *by* schools, *with* schools, and *for* schools in peer-driven networks of lateral pressure and support.

The student achievement results of schools in the *RATL* network were impressive. Two-thirds of the schools improved at double the rate of the national secondary school average in just two years (in terms of the percentage of students with a score of Grade C and above in the critical, high-stakes General Certificate of Secondary Education [GCSE] examination). Rather than demanding and imposing change *vertically*, *RATL* drove improvement *laterally* through heightened professional engagement and deepened professional inquiry and reflection. Specifically, *RATL* does the following:

- *Invites participation by underachieving schools*, which are identified by quantitative indicators of performance dips or declines in GCSE examination results, standardized test scores, and measures of value-added achievement.
- *Networks schools* through conferences and programs of intervisitation and exchange, so schools experiencing difficulties begin to learn from and support each other in their quest for improvement. They discover there are many others in the same boat, and realize that underperformance is a common challenge, not a symptom of individual inadequacy.
- *Makes mentor schools* and school leaders available to participants in the network as providers of coaching, support, and available solutions. Mentor schools are not assigned to struggling partners. Instead, a group of them displays their practices at *RATL* conferences so that participating schools can contact, visit, and communicate with them in their own way, at a time of their own choosing. The ethic of *RATL* is that the strong help the weak—by invitation and choice, not by compulsion and assignment. Importantly, mentor schools are offered compensatory resources so they do not lose capacity and performance as a consequence of devoting time to others.
- *Provides visionary inspiration and motivation* through speeches from outstanding school leaders and leading-edge thinkers at network conferences and through project leadership, which energizes schools in the change process by addressing the necessities of and achievable possibilities for improvement.
- *Supplies technical systems and assistance* for analyzing student achievement and other school-level data, especially in relation to

value-added measures and data that take into account factors in the local context, such as degrees of family and community deprivation, so that schools can target their improvement efforts more accurately and effectively.

- *Injects into the network an array of experience-driven and practically proven strategies*, of a short-, medium-, and long-term nature, for raising achievement and transforming learning. Network participants then apply those strategies to their own situations.
- *Incentivizes participation and improvement* through modest funding (equivalent to $16,000 per annum per school) to be spent entirely at the principal's or school's professional discretion in relation to improvement goals.
- *Uses technology effectively* to connect participating schools through a widely used Web portal and to link students across schools so they can exchange study strategies.
- *Establishes accountability through transparent processes* of participation as well as through public visibility of measured outcomes. Underachievement is numerically evident, and so too are the efforts that schools make to seek help in rectifying it. There is peer pressure as well as peer support.

Underlying and driving these strategies, *RATL* leaders have invented a unique and sophisticated model that yielded early and measurable benefits in student achievement in two-thirds of project schools. The model is practically based in experience, yet also intelligently informed by evidence. It values inside-outside engagement of development and research undertaken by, with, and for schools in energetic, peer-driven networks (rather than top-down impositions) focused on student learning. *RATL* combines a sense of urgency and a push for success with a culture of optimism and inspiration that leads educators to understand and appreciate that, with some outside assistance, the solutions to raising achievement lie within their own professional hands. *RATL* replaces the *fear* factor with the *peer* factor as the prime instigator and motivator of change.

The educators we interviewed were enthusiastic—indeed effusive—about the power of *RATL*'s support and interventions. They were grateful for assistance from *RATL* leaders in converting mountains of data into practical knowledge that could be acted on to improve student achievement. Especially when we visited schools with high numbers of students from poor and minority families, we were impressed by educators' accounts of the concrete recommendations and strategies they had gathered through *RATL*'s conferences, visits with mentor schools, and ideas exchanged on the online Web portal.

> The Assistant Head and I went together and we came away really, really enthusiastic because there were lots of practical hints, practical tips, things that if you took just one of them wasn't going to make a big difference, but if you pick and choose several and say, "how can I apply that to my school?" that was the way that we felt we could move.[10]

Almost 1,000 schools have now passed through the *RATL* networking process. The project demonstrates how networks can contribute to improvement, even when most participants are weak or struggling schools. It offers an alternative and an antidote to the strident strategies of ruthless competition and top-down reform in the Second Way and to the autocratically imposed improvement targets of the Third Way. It shows how successful networks are neither conduits for delivering government policy nor cultures of vague encouragement and unfocused interaction. Instead, they have specific design architectures and norms of participation that yield results. Here, at last, is a change network that recognizes how, with a little external organization and support, educators themselves can find and apply solutions in their own settings that produce demonstrable success!

Despite relentless prodding, educators had almost nothing negative to say about *RATL*, apart from the complaints about time constraints that afflict all school change efforts. The greatest challenges faced by *RATL* are largely due to the unchanging political context of high-stakes testing, top-down reform, and imposed initiatives in which it has had to operate. As we explained earlier, schools were understandably more enthusiastic and energetic about engaging with and adopting short-term strategies that yielded immediate results rather than with undertaking long-term transformation in teaching and learning. The project is now directly addressing this limitation with a cohort of schools where fundamental transformation is the priority.[11]

In the end, successful networks like *RATL* become more than an optional extra for the system or a device to implement its policies. They eventually challenge the logic of the system itself. They demonstrate the power of development over delivery, of professional responsibility over administrative accountability, and of energetic involvement over bureaucratic alignment.

THE DEMOCRATIC MOVEMENT

Educational policies have many purposes. They provide benefits to children and other learners. They advance the learning that the society needs to secure its future. They respond to crises, appease special interests, and keep the electorate satisfied. Policies rarely change because of advocacy or protests by professional groups alone. Only when these professional groups connect with more-powerful interests such as those in the business lobby, or when they mobilize public opinion, do professional causes have a chance of success.

Policymakers are not only shapers of public education but can also be obstructionists, blocking positive movements for educational change that are at odds with other parts of the political agenda and the interests they serve. On occasion, policymakers reduce budgets in line with the ideology of market fundamentalism or accede to the demands of powerful lobby groups whose interests conflict with those of children in schools.[12] In these circumstances, public activism and engagement in a district or a nation are needed to move the mountains that impede the path of improvement. In America, this approach to change is known as *community organizing*.[13] A little-understood and often bit-part player in social and educational reform, community organizing shot to national prominence when America's most famous community organizer, Barack Obama, was elected president in 2008.[14]

Community organizing in education goes far beyond parent involvement and its traditional one-on-one deals between individual parents and the educators who serve their children. It is about mobilizing entire communities and public networks to agitate for significant reform. When fully realized, it is about changing the power dynamics of an entire city by creating new civic capacity for previously disenfranchised populations.[15]

In the past, larger efforts to organize parents revealed they were often divided among themselves, incapable of galvanizing anything beyond episodic protests, and easily sidestepped in the political push for standardization and control. This pattern of fragmented and fractious engagement occurred within a dispiriting context of "diminished democracy" in which fewer Americans participated in the older forms of civic life and more preferred to contribute to large voluntary associations that represented their own single interests and did not involve them with a wider public committed to a more common good.[16] Moreover, it was easy for administrators to politically pick off parents who were anxious about their children's futures in a fast-paced age of uncertainty by arousing their nostalgia for schools as they used to be through back-to-basics policies in tested literacy and mathematics.[17]

Yet the tide is turning. The massive voter turnout in the 2008 presidential election among young, new, and minority voters is ample evidence of that. In addition to the prominence of community organizing within the U.S. president's political portfolio, a new wave of community and youth organizing, supported by powerful funders such as the Ford, Hazen, Mott, and Gates foundations, is getting beyond the "powerful reforms with shallow roots" that Michael Usdan and Larry Cuban decried as being endemic to American change efforts.[18]

- In New York City, the Community Collaborative to Improve District 9 Schools in the South Bronx developed a teacher support program with the city's public schools that reduced teacher attrition from 28% to 6.5% in targeted schools within a single year.[19]
- In Philadelphia, high school activists with "Youth United for Change" exposed how one of the only three secondary schools in the city that had achieved "Adequate Yearly Progress" had done so by teachers coaching students on test items and posting answers to anticipated test questions on walls when tests were administered.[20]
- In Chicago, the Logan Square Neighborhood Association and other community groups have created a "Grow Your Own" teacher preparatory program linked with area universities to prepare poor and working-class parents to become certified teachers.[21]

In these and other cases, community and youth organizers have moved beyond 1960s-style protest politics to conduct research with university allies, create and lead charter schools, provide professional development for teachers, and educate parents in how to collect evidence for change by combining data analyses of student achievement with in-class observations of teaching and learning.

One of us documented efforts by the Industrial Areas Foundation in Texas to turn around struggling urban schools in the 1990s.[22] These efforts developed a network of roughly 150 "Alliance Schools" that linked schools with faith-based institutions and community organizations. From inner-city Dallas and Fort Worth to the squalid *colonias* along the Rio Grande Valley, the Alliance Schools activated parents and teachers who improved student achievement, reconnected parents to the public school system, and improved community conditions from health care to housing and public safety. These promising efforts fell on hard times in Texas as increasing standardization and testing led principals to view working with parents as a distraction from the quest to meet their Adequate Yearly Progress targets. But larger lessons from the Alliance Schools spread to other cities and neighborhoods across the United States and contributed to the growth of community organizing as a new way to bring about educational change in the face of self-serving governments and obstructive bureaucracies.

Jeannie Oakes and John Rogers at the University of California, Los Angeles (UCLA), argue that conventional change and reform strategies fail because strategies for bringing about change are directed at and driven by education professionals with little involvement of students and parents other than as targets or recipients of the change effort.[23] In this sense, neither the means nor the ends of most change efforts, nor the theories of action that underpin them, challenge or confront the structures of power and control in society that systematically protect the schools, programs, and pedagogical strategies that are especially advantageous for elites and their children.

In response, Oakes and Rogers use community organizing to propose changes that raise achievement and secure wider improvement by connecting low-achieving poor and minority students and their families to university researchers and teacher networks. These groups train and support students and communities to inquire into and then act on the conditions of their own education and lives that include dilapidated school buildings, large class sizes, divisive tracking (streaming), inadequate books and materials, shortages of qualified teachers, and restricted opportunities for teachers to learn.

These practices are linked to an activist orientation among students, parents, and local communities who challenge bureaucrats and legislators with evidence-based arguments as well as disruptive strategies and knowledge, to provide genuinely equal opportunities for the poor as well as for the affluent. Faculty at UCLA supply expertise to community and youth organizing groups that ranges from high-level legal representation to the day-to-day politics of improving large urban high schools. In the words of an old Irish song, these strategies are "the wind that shakes the barley."

With the advent of Barack Obama as president, community organizing may be able to move from the margins to the mainstream of educational reform in the United States.[24] But what of its impact and effectiveness? In the most sophisticated large-scale study to date, an Annenberg Institute for School Reform research team has identified a number of positive outcomes of community organizing.[25] School district student achievement results, graduation rates, and enrollments in college preparatory courses were analyzed across seven urban districts to illuminate correlations between organizing strategies and measures of educational improvement.

- People Acting for Community Together (PACT) in Miami used a congregationally based organizing approach matching parents with partner schools to focus on literacy instruction in elementary schools. The schools improved from 27% students at proficiency in 2001 to 49% in 2005, far outpacing a demographically similar comparison set of schools in Grades 3 and 4.
- In Austin, Texas, schools with higher levels of teacher engagement in education organizing showed larger percentages of students meeting minimum standards on Texas's state test when controlled

for student socioeconomic status and limited English proficiency, and after controlling for the effect of baseline test scores.

- A campaign by the Oakland Community Organization broke up that city's largest and most dysfunctional high schools into small schools that subsequently showed increased graduation rates and enrollment levels in college-preparatory coursework, as well as improved ratings on California's Academic Performance Index.
- On a survey distributed across seven sites, young people who affiliated with education organizing projects reported a higher level of civic engagement than a national comparison group. Organizing experience was also a significant predictor of enhanced academic motivation.

Perhaps the most interesting finding of the Annenberg team was that community organizing is correlated with higher levels of social trust within schools, and between schools and community members. Previous research has found social trust in schools to be correlated with student achievement.[26] Surveys of teachers engaged in community organizing in Austin showed that schools that had high levels of involvement with Austin Interfaith had higher levels of teacher-parent trust, stronger senses of school community and safety, a more achievement-oriented culture, and greater degrees of parent involvement in school compared with schools with less involvement. High levels of community organizing were also associated with greater trust among teachers, commitment to their school, and professional collaboration. The survey data indicate that community and education organizing is associated with a dilution of the individualism among teachers that typically impedes improvement and achievement in schools.

The existence and effects of community organizing underline how positive educational change often starts beneath or beyond government policy. In church basements, on street corners, in union offices, and on the World Wide Web, community organizing is a dynamic part of public life and demonstrates how parents and communities can be so much more than objects of political intervention or recipients of government services. They can be citizens democratically engaged in educational change. Good governments are responsive to this activism. Even better governments create the conditions that extend it—developing the community's power and capacity to engage in and agitate for change as an essential element of democracy.

THE TURNED-AROUND DISTRICT

London's Docklands are squeezed into a tiny peninsula that occupies one of the last snaking bends of the River Thames before it opens out into the

English Channel.[27] Half a century ago, it was home to a white working-class community of dockworkers and their families who lived almost on top of each other in tightly packed terraced houses along cobblestone streets. The neighborhood was held together by the strong bonds and trusted kinship of extended family networks.[28]

In the 1950s and 1960s, postwar planners bulldozed away much of the old and bombed-out housing stock along with the street-corner spaces for congregating and building community that went with them. The old homes were replaced with low-quality tenements that separated families into isolated little boxes with no natural meeting places to gather and form relationships. In a few short years, these tenements became the graffiti-marked slums of the future, falling in to the same vicious circle of crime and alienation that afflicted U.S. housing projects.

Aspirational families from the Docklands found a way out. They bought their first cars and moved to promising new suburbs like Essex, where international soccer star David Beckham was raised. Meanwhile, modernism transformed the shipping industry, too. By the 1970s, a new generation of gigantic oil tankers and container ships could no longer navigate the Thames's hairpin bends. The docking industry was decimated, local employment dried up, and the traditional working class disintegrated, replaced first by an unemployed white underclass and then by immigrants from around the globe.

Many of the new wave of immigrants to the Docklands came from rural areas of Bangladesh, one of the world's poorest countries. Like generations of immigrants before, they came with extended family members; by the 1990s, the community was 50% Bangladeshi. Despite the reconstruction of part of the Docklands into the fashionable global finance and media center of Canary Wharf, the white-collar workers who came and went on the new high-tech transit line were barely aware of the immigrant community in their midst whose people found little skilled employment in the office towers of glass and steel.

These sweeping demographic changes were compounded by the tumultuous educational politics of the 1980s and early 1990s. When Margaret Thatcher broke up the left-leaning Inner London Education Authority, the borough of Tower Hamlets was one of many new authorities to emerge in its place. Tower Hamlets served the diverse multicultural community that suffered from high unemployment rates and some of the greatest incidences of poverty in the country, with more children on free school meals than almost anywhere else. Educators' aspirations for student achievement were startlingly low. In 1997, Tower Hamlets was proclaimed the country's worst-performing Local Education Authority, with the lowest-performing primary school in the nation.

Ten years later, the transformation of the schools in Tower Hamlets is dramatic. The schools perform around and above the national average. On standardized achievement tests, GCSE examination results, and rates of students going on to university, the borough ranks as the most improved local authority in Britain. It has significantly reduced achievement gaps in relation to children with special educational needs, those from cultural minorities, and those on free school meals. These gains have been achieved with largely the same population and are reflected in Figures 3.2 and 3.3 in relationship to the more modest national gains posted in the same period.

Figure 3.2   Secondary School Examination Results in Tower Hamlets

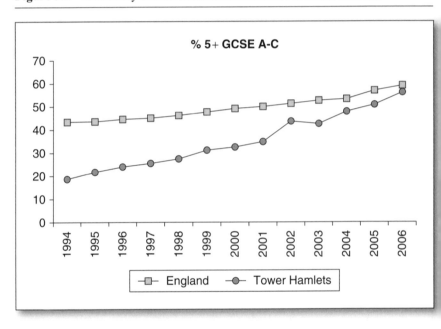

Note: Figure 3.2 refers to the percentage of students gaining five or more passing scores at Grade C and above in their crucial GCSE secondary school examinations. Grade C is typically the minimum required to move on to university-bound programs.

What explains this systemwide turnaround? How could achievement results improve so remarkably with a population that many had given up on, thinking they were beyond help or hope? In the large-scale research project, *Performing Beyond Expectations*, codirected with Alma Harris, one of us has been studying the secrets of Tower Hamlets' success with team member Alan Boyle. Community development is at the center of the story.

Figure 3.3   Primary School Literacy Achievement in Tower Hamlets

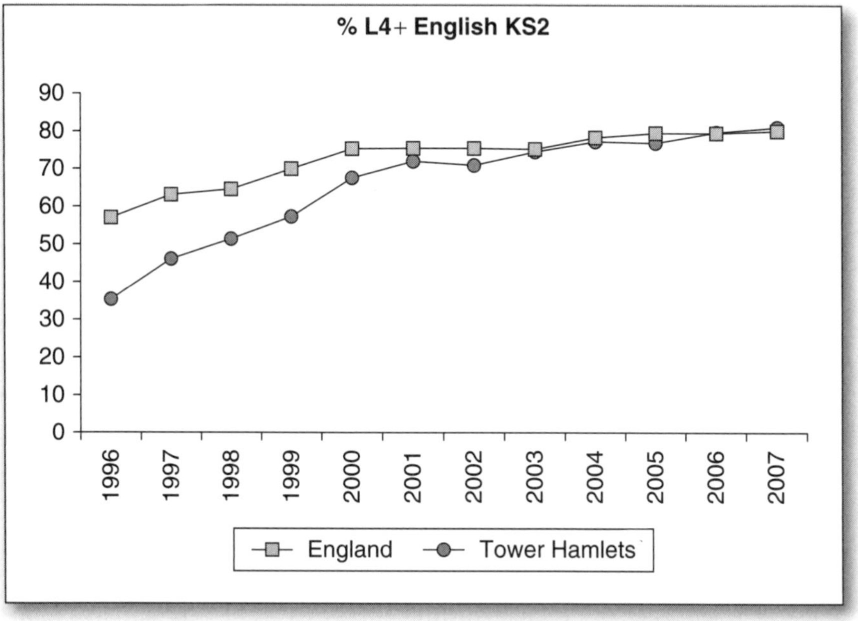

% L4+ English KS2

England   Tower Hamlets

Note: Figure 3.3 displays the percentage of students at key stage 2 (age 11/the last year of primary school) who attain level 4 proficiency in English literacy.

While England's Third Way has endeavored to *deliver* more children's services to disadvantaged and other communities, Tower Hamlets has worked tirelessly to *create new capacity* to strengthen community relations and engagement. It has done this by working with faith-based organizations and forming agreements with imams from this largely Muslim community to counter the effects of children taking extended absence from schools to attend and then stay on after family events such as funerals in Bangladesh. This includes announcements at school and at prayer in the mosque that extended absences will be treated as truancy because the educational achievement of the young people, and the development of the community's future capacity, matter that much.

Likewise, Tower Hamlets has developed some of its schools into community centers in a way that would have made John Dewey proud— establishing extended services that keep a school open from 8:00 a.m. until 10:00 p.m., providing resources and recreation for both students and the community's adults. Like the "wraparound services" piloted in a few American cities, Tower Hamlets has created new synergies of support and learning in schools where health services and the support services of student learning mentors are combined on one integrated site.

This recalls and re-creates a fine tradition of community development in Britain that was formed during the First Way of educational and social change. At that time, innovative comprehensive secondary schools such as the community colleges of Leicestershire, Stantonbury Campus in Milton Keynes, and Sidney Stringer Community College in Coventry operated as some of the first urban community schools. They were open all hours to students and community members; they integrated educational services for young people with library, leisure, family, child care, and continuing education services for adults; and they focused key parts of the project-based curriculum on local community concerns.[29]

One important factor that has strengthened community engagement in Tower Hamlets has been the impact of legislation known as "workforce remodeling."[30] This legislation was designed to place more classroom assistants and other staff in schools to support teachers by taking over some of their administrative and other tasks. Existing research wisdom would have suggested this might not be an effective strategy. In a classic gold-standard study in Tennessee, using experimental and control groups, one set of teachers was allocated smaller classes while teachers in a comparison group were each assigned a classroom assistant.[31] Those who were allocated assistants performed less well than those with smaller classes.

However, the Tennessee study was undertaken in snapshots of time, on the technical assumption that modifying just one of the variables that influence classroom management and effectiveness would reveal which strategy to adopt systemwide. Cumulatively and longitudinally, though, workforce remodeling has come to mean that around half the adults in many schools in England now come from the community itself. They are not "qualified" teachers based on the criteria established by the government, but they have proven themselves to be superb "street-level democrats" who develop strong relationships with the teachers and leaders of the school and sometimes go on to become professionally trained teachers themselves.[32] As one Tower Hamlets leader commented, "We've got quite strong training and development opportunities for local people [who] particularly come through as teaching assistants in our schools to train up to become teachers so I think we've got a good way of delivering more home grown teachers and social workers." These groups of professionals and employees from the local community, working alongside each other for the students they share in common, build communities of active trust, engagement, and advocacy that bring about improvement. One leader stated that it was about "creating those links and making sure everybody feels part of one community and they have access."

So Tower Hamlets used community development strategies to recognize and develop indigenous community leadership, strengthen trusting relationships between professionals and community members, and transform schools into vibrant examples of democracy. In this way, the district was far from being just one more site for the government's "deliverology."[33] These processes of community development operated in synergy with other transformational elements of the district's improvement agenda:

- The *visionary leadership* of a new director (superintendent) who was a self-confessed workaholic and who believed that "poverty is not an excuse for poor outcomes," that aspirations should be extremely high, that efforts to meet these aspirations should be relentless, and that everyone should work on these goals together
- The *successful succession* of this first driving leader by a more developmentally inclined yet equally persistent leader, with just a short period of instability in between
- The ability to attract *high-quality teachers who stay* with the school district, after a period of weeding out overseas teachers who were drawn more to enjoying a brief excursion in London than to a long-term professional commitment to the schools
- A commitment developed with the schools' leaders to set and reach ambitious *shared targets* for improvement in "a culture of target setting" so that "everybody owns them"
- A shared philosophy that *it is better to have ambitious targets and just miss them than have more modest targets and meet them*
- *Mutual trust and strong respect* where "lots of our schools work very closely together and with the local authority" and where inspectors' reports refer to the "enthusiasm and high level of morale among the workforce"
- *Knowledge of and presence in the schools* that provide support, build trust, and ground intervention in consistent and direct personal knowledge and communication more than in the numerical data that eventually appear on spreadsheets
- A commitment to *cross-school collaboration*, so that when one secondary school went into "Special Measures" (similar to "corrective action" in the United States) after taking in Somali students from refugee families in a neighboring authority, all the other secondary schools rallied round to help
- A *resilient but not reckless* approach to external government pressure and policy—accepting the importance of testing and targets but deciding to set their own targets and resisting the politically motivated pressure to build new high school academies since the

authority already had high-trust relationships with its schools that now performed very well

- The economic regeneration of sections of Canary Wharf that has created an environment of hope and well-being through *positive business partnerships* that model a new form of "corporate educational responsibility" with schools

Here, community development penetrates all aspects of a cohesive and coherent change process, while enhancing and not displacing the special expertise of educators in boosting achievement. Educators in Tower Hamlets possess a robust and resilient sense of purpose, enjoy successful and sustainable system leadership that stays close to and is undertaken with schools, commit to professionally shared rather than politically arbitrary targets, and establish an ethic of schools helping schools and the strong supporting the weak. In the Fourth Way of change, talented and courageous leaders will know how to capitalize on these partnerships and engagements between professionals and communities in order to build the civic capacity within our towns and cities that increases student achievement.

Good governments do not merely tolerate and endure community organizing as a regrettable and dispensable distraction from learning. Rather, they respectfully and continuously engage with parents and community activists to promote wider change strategies. More than this, they create the preconditions that enable community organizing to flourish as an essential element of change and a key component of local and national democracy that is sustainable beyond any one term of government office. Workforce remodelling created a new public identity for Bangladeshis who could have been all too easily marginalized from educational improvement through a narrow, bureaucratic, and in some ways ethnocentric definition of teacher quality. Such progressive policies enable us to understand that, in the end, the moral task of democratic governments and their advisors is not to do what is easy, politically convenient, or popular, but to know how to capitalize on these community-based initiatives and capabilities in order to build the civic capacity that increases student achievement. One of Tower Hamlets' visionary leaders sums it up well: "[It's] not just about the data. It's actually knowing the school, knowing the community, knowing about history, knowing about the staff—all of that."

CONCLUSION

When we combine what we can learn from Finland *beside* the Third Way, the *RATL* network *beyond* it, and community organizing and development *betwixt* it, we start to see the emergence of powerful new principles of improvement. These new principles start to delineate a *Fourth Way* of change that will bring together an energized profession with an engaged public and a guiding but not controlling government, in an interactive partnership of equals dedicated to serving and improving the public and educational common good. These principles include the importance of

- a compelling, inclusive, and inspirational vision in the society and its schools;
- learning and achievement priorities that follow the vision;
- attraction and retention of high-quality teachers;
- professional cultures of trust, cooperation, and responsibility;
- evidence-informed rather than data-driven improvement;
- close relationships of mutual trust between districts and schools;
- professional networking of peers and with mentors;
- cultures of improvement where the strong help the weak; and
- community development, engagement, and empowerment.

The Second Way of markets and standardization and the Third Way's New Orthodoxy of performance-driven targets and testing can take us no further forward when trust in the free-market system has collapsed, individual insecurity abounds, and when we need to rally all of our collective resources to building the common good. Our future must depend no longer on the unfettered freedoms of market fundamentalism or on the arrogance of autocratic government control. It must reside in developing the present and future capacities of one another and must depend on investing in and trusting the high-quality professional expertise that can help us. The solutions for tomorrow cannot be based on retreats to or incremental reinventions of those that have already failed us. In the midst of this great historical turning, at a momentous time of crisis and opportunity, we must face and embrace dramatic transformations in our habits and beliefs, rediscover the best of what is inside us, and connect it to a greater good beyond ourselves as we sacrifice and strive for a better future together. This is the great promise and profound challenge of *the Fourth Way*.

— ■■ —

They must often change, who would be constant
in happiness or wisdom.

—CONFUCIUS

All change is a miracle to contemplate; but it is a
miracle which is taking place every second.

—HENRY DAVID THOREAU

CHAPTER FOUR

THE FOURTH WAY

The Six Pillars of Purpose

The Three Principles of Professionalism

The Four Catalysts of Coherence

T*he Fourth Way* is a way of inspiration and innovation, of responsibility and sustainability. The Fourth Way does not drive reform relentlessly through teachers, use them as final delivery points for government policies, or vacuum up their motivations into a vortex of change defined by short-term political agendas and the special interests with which they are aligned. Rather, it brings together government policy, professional involvement, and public engagement around an inspiring social and educational vision of prosperity, opportunity, and creativity in a world of greater inclusiveness, security, and humanity.

The Fourth Way pushes beyond standardization, data-driven decision making, and target-obsessed distractions to forge an equal and interactive partnership among the people, the profession, and their government. It enables educational leaders to "let go" of the details of change, steering broadly whenever they can and intervening directly only when they must—to restore safety, avoid harm, and remove incompetence and corruption from the system.

The Fourth Way involves a trade-off for educators. It releases teachers from the tightened grip of government control. It also reduces their autonomy from parents, communities, and the public. Parents become more involved in the daily lives of their children's education, community members become more visible and vocal in schools, and the public gets engaged in determining the purposes of education together rather than simply consuming the services that are delivered to them.

In Linda Darling-Hammond's terms, the Fourth Way brings about change through democracy and professionalism rather than through bureaucracy and the market. It transfers trust and confidence back from the discredited free market of competition among schools and reinvests them in the expertise of highly trained and actively trusted professionals.[1] At the same time, it reduces political bureaucracy while energizing public democracy. This means a fundamental shift in teachers' professionalism that restores greater autonomy from government and introduces more openness to and engagement with parents and communities. The Fourth Way, therefore, means significant change for everyone—governments, parents, and teacher unions alike (see Figure 4.1).

Figure 4.1   The Fourth Way

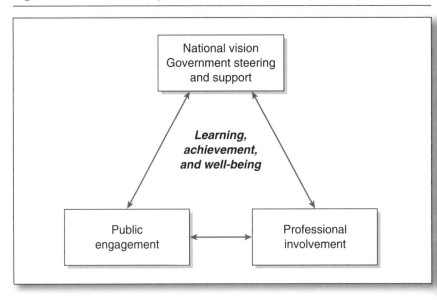

This chapter lays out the new theory-of-action of the Fourth Way—a Way more suited than previous Ways to building prosperous and competitive knowledge societies, to removing injustice and inequity, to restoring professional expertise and integrity, and to establishing greater cohesion and inclusion in our communities and societies than any of its predecessors. It consists of

- six pillars of purpose and partnership that support change,
- three principles of professionalism that drive change, and
- four catalysts of coherence that sustain change and hold it together.

SIX PILLARS OF PURPOSE AND PARTNERSHIP

Any theory of action of sustainable change must rest on the original meaning of the Latin verb *sustinere*, to sustain. To sustain means not merely to *maintain* or *endure*, but also to *hold up* or to *bear the weight of* something. What will ultimately bear the weight of sustainable educational change is not an overarching set of bureaucratic policies and interventions that shift from one government to the next, that subject educators to repetitive change syndrome and that undermine the basic trust and confidence that support their relationships with students. Data can enhance and inform these relationships but cannot replace the value of teachers working closely and effectively with students and colleagues, students learning from and supporting each other, and all of them engaging with parents and communities around purposes they develop and deliberate on together.

Research on happiness, including our own, backs this up. The three things that most make people happy are purposes, power, and relationships.[2] Teachers feel positive emotions when their *purposes* are clear, focused, and achievable, and when those purposes belong to them. They become unhappy when purposes are vague, scattered, unrealistic, constantly changing, or are imposed by someone else. Second, teachers, like other people, feel happy when they experience being *empowered*, in control of their work lives and not at the beck and call of others. Last, happiness comes from developing and achieving purposes in positive *relationships* with colleagues and others, whereas unhappiness springs from a professional life that provides no time to develop or sustain any relationships at all. Inspiring purposes developed and achieved with others are the foundation of successful and sustainable educational change.

In the Fourth Way, there are *six pillars of purpose and partnership*. These are

- an inspiring and inclusive vision;
- strong public engagement;
- achievement through investment;
- corporate educational responsibility;
- students as partners in change; and
- mindful learning and teaching.

1. AN INSPIRING AND INCLUSIVE VISION

At the start of the week, during a bout of union action when teachers follow their contract to the letter and arrive at school just minutes before lessons start, you come in early, warm up the photocopiers, and get everything ready for them—only to have letters of grievance slapped on your desk the next day on the instructions of the union. You spend your own money helping a troubled youth on Wednesday, then discover he has skipped parole on Thursday. You advise colleagues to try a new software program to track students' grades on Friday and are bombarded by emails on Saturday and Sunday complaining that the program has crashed. Finally, the new report card that you and your staff spent months developing is made redundant by yet another government replacement the month after.

Many educators get bogged down by these petty setbacks. Some work to the point of exhaustion. They become moral martyrs who try to fix everything themselves—every misbehaving student, all the paperwork, and every backed-up toilet or parent complaint. They have to be first in, last out every day. This demonstrates impressive dedication but it comes at an enormous cost because it leaves no time to address the bigger picture. These educators are good at putting out fires, but they never have time to find out who's starting the fires in the first place.

Others, however, are able to bounce back from adversity. They have what psychologists call *resilience*—from the Latin *resilere*, to react back. These educators rebound from and even thrive on threats and challenges that defeat colleagues elsewhere. Even the best reform environments bring frustration and adversity. Unwanted reforms are replaced by uncoordinated initiatives and opportunities. Declining enrollments give way to classroom overcrowding. There's always something to complain about. It's resilient people who turn problems into opportunities and "lemons into lemonade."

Two of the key predictors of resilience are a strong sense of purpose and a supportive partnership.[3] Individuals who have a sense of inner purpose and moral vision have the drive to get beyond grievances by redefining them as challenges that can be overcome or opportunities to improve. Research on children in poverty reveals that those who can extricate themselves from it have at least one trusted adult on whom they can rely for help. It's easier to be resilient when you know that there is someone—*even just one person*—who is on your side.[4]

Resilient teachers are able to synthesize and streamline standards so they suit their own curriculum purposes. One resilient teacher in the *Change Over Time* study turned an unwanted Second Way reform requirement for youngsters to have compulsory work experience into an opportunity to build a garden together around the perimeter of the school building—a haven of creativity in a context of almost unbearable political constraint. Like the visionary administrators in Tower Hamlets and persistent community organizers across America, resilient leaders in challenging circumstances know how to get parents and communities on their side and fight the inflexible bureaucracies that hold them back.[5]

Schools can be resilient, too. Innovative schools with a distinctive purpose are used to having embattled identities that they define and defend against unsympathetic superiors. One school in the *Change Over Time* study circumvented the restrictive state examinations by securing a waiver to undertake performance-based assessments with a statewide network of schools that it cofounded. Others used district training and implementation days to develop their own site-based purposes and priorities. Finally, one school even drew a full house at every staff meeting by beginning with a puppet show in which a talking fish hilariously satirized the more bizarre aspects of the government's latest reform pronouncements, before the staff moved on to adapt those selfsame reforms to their own improvement agenda.

Countries can be surprisingly resilient, too. We have already described Finland's remarkable economic and educational transformation. Nearby Baltic states are rebounding just as impressively from half a century of communist stagnation and oppression. Germany is no longer divided by a wall. Japan transformed itself from a broken military power to a global economic one. Singapore was economically off the map as recently as the 1960s but is now a leading economic and educational knowledge economy. Once a far-flung destination for Anglo-Saxon emigration, Australia is today a leading cosmopolitan nation and entrepreneurial power in the Asia-Pacific region. Finally, Obama now stands alongside Mandela as an improbable black leader his country would finally have.

American "exceptionalists" have looked at the successes of countries like Finland and Singapore and then thrown up their hands, saying the United States just isn't like them.[6] They have stuck with habitual frames of reference emphasizing individualism, markets, and competition as the solutions of choice for all new and emerging challenges. Even after the cataclysmic credit crisis of 2008, many held fast to outdated ideological beliefs that financial analysts around the globe had urged them to abandon years before the crisis peaked.[7] In the rapidly changing 21st century, America's new challenge is not to be an exception, but to be exceptional.

Contrary to the biblical proverb on accepting things as they are, leopards really can change their spots! Indeed, when the environment changes, leopards' survival may depend on their ability to adapt. Internationally, country after country has responded to change by transforming its identity—connecting a different future to the best of its past. Entrepreneurially, Japanese car companies such as Honda and Toyota were the first to market smaller vehicles during the oil crisis of the 1970s and the first into the hybrid vehicle market from the 1990s, while American companies stood by and watched. The collapse of the U.S. auto giants in 2008 repeats this tragic historical pattern of management failures to learn from more-flexible business practices elsewhere.

Now the credit crunch is on, and with climate change–induced storm surges raging more furiously with every passing season, people are finally coming out of their consumer cocoons. America is starting to come back together after years of falling apart. Crises bring opportunity as well as calamity. When international banking systems collapsed in 2008, manufacturers of safes for storing cash could hardly keep up with demand. Increasing unemployment in the private sector prompts many highly qualified people to move into teaching. And it's not just the job security that attracts them. Having lost everything in a period of egocentric advancement, many individuals rediscover the deeper and more important purposes of work and life, and reconnect with each other in the process. People start to see how government support is necessary for everyone's security and that freedom from taxation at any cost cannot be defended. We all long for an inspiring purpose that connects us to each other and to an ideal that is greater than ourselves. It is especially at dramatic turning points like the present that the acquisitive push for money and property give way to this greater search for meaning.

A compelling and inclusive moral purpose steers a system, binds it together, and draws the best people to work in it. Literacy and numeracy are sometimes such a purpose and should always be an educational priority. But they are not always the right reform priority, especially when schools and nations are already high performers in those areas, or when they sideline other emphases that need more attention. For instance, while Canada ranks very high on tested literacy achievement and on economic prosperity as measures of educational well-being, it performs very poorly in self, family, peer-related, or health-based well-being.[8]

Raising the bar and closing the gap in tested literacy and mathematics is too narrow a goal.[9] Admittedly, if the goalposts are too far apart and there is too much to aim at, the bar will sag. If the posts are too close together, however, the bar will eventually topple because the focus is too narrow. The challenge is to address more than one thing in particular, without addressing everything at once.

Too much of the Anglo-American world has lost its wider sense of mission. Nowhere is this more evident than in education. England, among other countries, can only make vague and vacuous calls for "world-class education" and "world-class performance."[10] This is not an articulation of a vision, but rather an evasion of one. George W. Bush's America held out the individualistic prospect of an ownership society in which, it turned out, most people discovered they were on their own, and owned only their debts. Even calculations of achievement gaps are technical reductions and euphemistic evasions of the more inspiring and inclusive visions of social justice that bring people together in a spirit of equity and solidarity.

In schools and in societies, the locus of change is very often only tested literacy and numeracy. Where literacy and math scores are low and achievement gaps are wide, as in many parts of the United States or in many developing countries, this is an understandable priority, especially when linked with a broader repertoire of strategies to battle poverty and increase civic capacity. It makes no educational sense, however, for places such as Australia, New Zealand, or Ontario and British Columbia in Canada to make tested literacy their systemic reform priority when they already rank among the highest literacy performers in the world. These imported priorities from less-successful systems and their accompanying baggage of targets and testing may be politically expedient, but they are educationally misdirected. The courage of leadership, including political leadership, is not to do what is easy or expedient, but to do what is right.

So what might the inspiring mission be? There is no single answer. It might be innovation and creativity in societies that aspire to be knowledge societies or in indigenous communities that have always cultivated the arts. It may be gender equity in parts of the world that have denied women's basic human rights. In the U.S., there is a resurgent commitment to international partnerships among equals abroad and increased opportunities for everyone at home. Where societies have been torn apart by genocide and are still riven with ethnic tension, nonviolent conflict resolution may need to be secured before anything else. Or perhaps education for sustainable development should be the goal in regions with imperiled ancient ecologies, or in nations and cities that leave large ecological footprints.

In every nation, children deserve a curriculum that is varied, complex, challenging, and deep.[11] Every child has what Simone Weil, in the aftermath of World War II, called "the need for roots" that can ground them in their own traditions while opening their hearts and minds to other cultures around them. Basics are a beginning, but why should we stop there?[12] We need to be bolder and get better by moving beyond the basics.

2. STRONG PUBLIC ENGAGEMENT

The purposes that define a society's future vision should not be just for governments to decide. They are a matter for public engagement of citizens and community members and of leaders who can tap into and elevate public spiritedness. They have been central to the rise of the community organizing that Barack Obama has made famous.[13] They were a crucial component in turning around Tower Hamlets. Educators today work in a public profession, not a separate and sequestered one. Every time they meet with a concerned parent or discuss the future of their community with business or other leaders, educators have opportunities to influence public discourse and democratic deliberation about the achievements and aspirations of public education. House visits, home meetings, breakfast clubs, drama and athletic events, homework assignments shared with a family member, after-school activities, and parent-friendly meetings to discuss children's progress—these are all opportunities to help individual children and to strengthen public engagement in building a better system for other people's children, too.

When facing the future, anxiety without information makes people nostalgic for past certainties, turns them against progress and change, and leads them to clutch at the straws of test scores as substitutes for richer relationships that concern their own children. Informed public engagement and community development combat nostalgia by increasing involvement and understanding. This means developing a more open, civic professionalism that includes the public and then builds better schools together.

- Parents and students at one of the innovative schools in the *Change Over Time* study paraded in strait jackets outside the district office to protest the increased testing that threatened the richness of their learning and the distinctiveness of their school.
- Parents and community members in the Alliance Schools network held massive rallies at the Texas state house to urge legislators to support a Capital Investment Fund that provided additional resources for schools working with community-based organizations in promising and innovative ways.
- Western Australia dedicates one week a year to education— "Education Week"—sharing positive stories about public education in the media and in communities.
- The province of Ontario reached an agreement with the press not to mislead public opinion by converting complex school performance data into one-dimensional rankings.[14]
- In America and England, extended service or community schools are open all hours to provide after-school classes; courses in adult literacy, leisure, and parenting; facilities for homework; support and instruction for teenage parents and working mothers; and one-stop access to medical care, social work, and law enforcement services.
- Tower Hamlets and other urban local authorities in England created more jobs in schools for community members. This not only supported students and teachers, but also strengthened relationships with families and faith-based organizations, and increased everyone's commitments to improving achievement and attendance.

Educators need not fear parent activism and community development. They can and must learn to engage with and benefit from it as a core part of their professional calling and identity. Historically, the effects of families, communities, and society on student achievement and opportunity have been far greater than the effects of the schools.[15] Connecting schools more to their communities can reverse these patterns—increasing the school's influence *through* the community, not *aside from* or *against* it. Half a century and more ago, educational leaders were also community leaders. In small towns and rural areas, many still are. It is time for them to become leaders of and with their communities again. This new partnership and engagement must take place in individual schools, with local communities, and in invigorated national debates about the very purposes of public education.The passive trust between teachers and communities in the First Way and the active mistrust of teachers by parents and communities in the Second Way must now be superseded. And this must be done not through the increased public confidence about achievement results that characterizes the Third Way, but by the active trust that develops when professionals work side by side with parents and communities to serve the children and youth they care for together.

3. ACHIEVEMENT THROUGH INVESTMENT

The arrival of the 21st century was marked by a shift from shared social responsibility to support and create better opportunities for the poor, to an expectation that schools and teachers almost entirely alone should raise all students' achievement and narrow the gaps between them. The wider discourse of social equality degenerated into a demand that schools should close numerical achievement gaps by themselves.[16] Responsibility was lifted from the wider society and placed exclusively on schools. No excuses! Failure is not an option!

However, as we have just seen, years of research in school effectiveness still show that most explanations for differences in student outcomes exist *outside* the school.[17] Schools can and do make a significant difference but do not make all or even most of it. They cannot excel alone but need communities and society to work with and alongside them. This means more schools working with communities and more investment in community and family development.

We can't expect to raise standards on the cheap. In schools as in business, there is no achievement without investment. High-performing Finland and other Nordic countries benefit from a welfare state that makes strong public investment not just in education, but also in housing, medical care, social services, and community development. While schools contribute a great deal, they are not expected to achieve miracles by themselves.

The importance of investment is most spectacularly evident in developing and transitional economies like South Africa and in some of the poorest communities in the United States. In South Africa's former schools for privileged white children, literacy standards compare favorably with those in places like Germany or the United States. But in the schools that are in the black townships or where children live in extreme poverty, the literacy rates are among the lowest in the world.[18]

U.S. students are similarly split in a bimodal distribution of achievement and opportunity. White and Asian-American students do as well as high-performing international peers on tests like the OECD Programme for International Student Assessment (PISA) and the Trends in International Mathematics and Science Study (TIMSS), while their black and Latino counterparts too often suffer from poverty, unqualified teachers, and underfunded schools.[19] Malnutrition, untreated infant health concerns, hearing and sight problems, environmental pollutants that attack the brain, and fetal alcohol and drug-dependency difficulties all impair learning, sometimes for life.[20] Interestingly, countries such as the United Kingdom and United States that score poorly on the GINI index (the index of economic inequality that measures how wealth is distributed across a society) also rank poorly on international tests of educational achievement. Countries such as Canada and Finland with strong GINI scores perform much better educationally.[21]

The British "Schools for the Future" strategy seeks to change these patterns of ingrained inequality.[22] This disruptive innovation invests millions of pounds in rebuilding all the secondary schools in some of the country's most troubled towns and cities, to use them as a point of community regeneration as well as combating racism. The United States' full-service schools offer a step in the same direction.

None of this is merely a repeat of the First Way's unconditional state investment. The famous Iron Rule of community organizing that we cited previously is that one *never, ever should do for others what they can do for themselves*.[23] Parents and community members must step up to the plate, too. It's time to turn off the cell phone, TV, and DVD, to take the time to talk to children, to read to them, and to play with them. It's time to match greater professional accountability in the school with increased parental responsibility at home. It's time for communities to take back the playgrounds and the streets as part of the very fabric of democratic life.

4. CORPORATE EDUCATIONAL RESPONSIBILITY

In the past, corporate partners in education have often been negligent, shallow, and self-serving. Corporations have urged school systems to do skill-specific training so their businesses don't have to. They have exploited children as captive consumers and plied harmful products such as junk food as the price of their investment.[24] They have crowded critical thinking out of the curriculum by promoting functional business communication and business math rather than programs of study that are more challenging.[25] They are even behind the present push to develop twenty-first century skills to boost the global economy, while failing to advocate for the qualities and capacities in young people that develop civic engagement and humanitarian democracy. Such businesses promise investments in education when times are good, but slash those investments at the first signs of an economic downturn.

The environmental movement has challenged and led to shifts in many corporations' sense of their responsibilities. More and more businesses now practice corporate social responsibility. They take pride in where they rank on the Dow Jones Sustainability Index and in the practices that qualify them to be listed on it—reducing their emissions that affect the environment, improving the quality of life for their employees, and contributing time and service to their communities, including to the communities' schools.[26] Nokia Communications holds this status and influence in Finland. Similarly, the partnerships that the great financial and media institutions of Canary Wharf have forged with the schools of Tower Hamlets are designed not to promote particular products, but to offer a genuine service, enhance corporate status, and share some of the institutions' profits and largesse. When corporate *social* responsibility engages with social justice and educational opportunity in this way, it becomes corporate *educational* responsibility.

Positive and mutually beneficial partnerships also exist in developing countries, as one of us found in an evaluation of World Bank initiatives in knowledge and skills development.[27] The Peruvian asparagus industry, for example, treats local, indigenous knowledge as an asset for and not a barrier to economic development. This knowledge is disseminated in a public agricultural university where most of the industry's entrepreneurs are trained. Many of these entrepreneurs were brought to the United States by USAID to learn new techniques from U.S. asparagus growers and processors, while others learned about irrigated desert agriculture by taking courses in Israel. Technology was transferred to and then adapted for Peruvian conditions. The asparagus producers' association disseminates information and assists with marketing. In addition, the university produces and disseminates research on new export crops and on pest and disease control to technicians, large growers, and small farmers.

In Indonesia, one of Unilever's soap factories treats water from the nearby river to manufacture soap, toothpaste, and shampoo—since they all require clean water. It is in the company's commercial interest to improve water quality, and part of its social and environmental responsibility. Unilever Indonesia's "Clean River" program focuses on involving and training everybody living along the river to contribute to its improvement. This program provides training so that the villagers can look after the river in a self-sustaining way.

These cases show how local indigenous knowledge can enhance economic and social development when it is linked to public and private partnerships in education and training. The same is true in the apparent urban desolation of cities in the richest economies. The seemingly abandoned church basement is where the homeless are fed and the spirits of destitute families restored. Street corners are turned into places for people to gather and move beyond airing grievances into developing strategies for community organizing. Dilapidated schools can attract grants and donations for improving parenting skills or helping teenage mothers cope. During his organizing years in Chicago, Barack Obama showed how small businesses and employment centers can be resurrected to reignite entrepreneurialism and opportunity, as well as more than a little hope within the local community.[28]

Corporate educational responsibility demands a new kind of accountability. In partnerships between education and business, accountability becomes mutual and transparent, not secret and one sided. In state, provincial, and national governments as well as in local towns and communities, the businesses that approach or get invited to the educational policy and investment table should be those that exemplify or at least aspire to corporate educational and social responsibility. Codes of practice already exist as a basis for business partnerships in many schools and districts. They now need to extend to large-scale politics.

5. STUDENTS AS PARTNERS IN CHANGE

Students are usually the targets of change efforts and services. Rarely are they change partners. Students are highly knowledgeable about the things that help them learn—teachers who know their material, care for them, have a sense of humor, and never give up on them, for example.[29] Finnish schools work very well, in part because children are expected and prepared to be responsible from an early age.[30] Finnish schools are remarkably calm, with quiet and respectful relationships between students and teachers. The innovative schools in the *Change Over Time* project gave a prominent role to the students in their midst. And in one turnaround school in the *Performing Beyond Expectations* project that had been situated at the heart of communities where some of Britain's worst race riots had taken place, it was the students who said that the school's subsequent improvements would be sustainable because they ultimately belonged to them. Always remember: Without students, there would be no teachers. Their voices matter a lot.

Students' involvement in change in the *Raising Achievement, Transforming Learning (RATL)* network begins with assessment-for-learning strategies that require students to take responsibility for their own learning. School leaders are adamant that the data they gather "have to be personalized" for their learners. This leads students to become more reflective about what and how they learn best, shows their teachers how to help them, and enables them to negotiate next steps and set progress targets with their teachers for the future.

Students can also be involved in changing their peers, often in ways that are as powerful as those that are used by their teachers. They can play with or read to young children in earlier grades. They can serve as mentors for struggling students in high school and assist students in other schools with study skills on the Web. They can stand up together for children who are bullied and learn valuable life skills as mediators who teach others how to resolve conflicts without violence.

Being partners in change also means being involved in school and district decision making. This includes obvious areas such as contributing to the design of new behavior codes, but it also includes being part of school improvement planning, of professional development days that focus on school change, and of appointing principals and other leaders in schools. Boston Public Schools even include young people in negotiating teachers' contracts. In urban environments throughout the United States, new youth organizing groups are giving young people fresh skills to advocate for improvements in teacher quality and college preparatory courses.[31]

Last but not least, if schools and school systems sustain a broader vision, and express it in their teaching and curricula, students will become more interested in and committed to changing the world. Young people crave opportunities not just to react and obey, but also to lead and create a better future. Democratic engagement of young people must not end with their remarkable and resurgent involvement in political elections. Their engagement must be encouraged and enabled to spread throughout their learning and their lives. What finer theory of action could there be than one that creates millions of change agents for the future?

6. MINDFUL LEARNING AND TEACHING

A central educational strategy of Third Way reformers has been "personalized learning." Announced by the U.K. Labor government's former minister, David Miliband, advanced by Sir Michael Barber, and now increasingly advocated in the United States, personalized learning is supposed to tailor teaching and assessment to the strengths, needs, and learning styles of individual students.[32] For U.K. change guru David Hargreaves, personalization is realized in

[a]n articulate, autonomous but collaborative learner, with high metacognitive control and the generic skills of learning

gained through engaging educational experiences with enriched opportunities and challenges, and supported by various people, materials and ICT [information and communication technology] linked to general well-being but crucially focused on learning in schools whose cultures sustain the continuous construction of education through shared leadership.[33]

Full personalization, he continues, "demands a new shape for schooling" with a more rigorous emphasis on projects rather than the ubiquitous short lesson as the unit of learning.[34]

Here, the theme of personalization echoes the long-standing emphasis on what European educators call "lifelong learning," which is the highest realization of human potential.[35] In this understanding, lifelong learning is not merely learning beyond school, throughout life, but also learning *about* life and *for* life. Lifelong learning is learning that develops lives and shapes the world. The lifelong learner is one who has initiative, is a problem solver, is creative and innovative in making the most of life chances, and contributes to the greater good.

But for David Hargreaves, personalization, like so many promising Third Way strategies, is sometimes equated with "the movement from mass production to mass customization."[36] Indeed, he initially referred to personalization in terms of "its synonym, customization in the business world."[37] With *customized learning*, students access existing and unchanged kinds of conventional learning through different means—on site or off site, online or offline, in school or out of school, quickly or slowly, cooperatively or alone. But the nature of the learning itself is not transformed into something deeper, more challenging, and more connected to compelling issues in their world and their lives. Customization becomes a tool to market and manage learning—not to develop or deepen it, which Hargreaves is now seeking to do in his most recent work.

Some aspects of the *RATL* network of underperforming schools exemplified this conversion of personalization into customization. Students could meet with their academic "progress managers" every few weeks to set targets and review their progress, but the nature of the learning itself often remained the same. Like choosing the colors of your cell phone, the play list on your iPod, or the options on your new car, customized learning is pleasurable and instantly gratifying. Nevertheless, it falls short of lifelong learning in the fullest sense and ultimately becomes just one more process of business-driven training delivered to satisfy individual consumer tastes and desires.

For the Fourth Way to achieve its high moral purposes, it must recover and reinvent the fullest meaning of personalization as learning for, through, and about life. It must reconceptualize the fundamental nature of teaching and learning itself, and not just the mechanisms for delivering it. The vital 21st-century skills that will drive new knowledge economies are integral to the agenda of personalized learning.[38] Creativity, innovation, intellectual agility, teamwork, problem solving, flexibility, and adaptability to change are essential to the new economy. But if these skills are all there is to 21st-century schools, they will convert personalization into mere customization in a fast-forward world of swift solutions and temporary teamwork.

Twenty-first-century schools must also embrace deeper virtues and values such as courage, compassion, service, sacrifice, long-term commitment, and perseverance. Otherwise, as acclaimed public intellectual Zygmunt Bauman warns us, flexibility will become little more than a synonym for spinelessness.[39]

Although neither of us is Catholic, the university where we work is a Jesuit institution that advances and embraces what is known as Jesuit pedagogy. When undergraduates first arrive at Boston College, they attend an opening lecture that challenges them to engage with three questions that should animate their entire liberal arts education:

- Do you have a passion?
- Are you good at it, or can you become so?
- Does it serve a compelling social need?

If your answer to all three questions is "Yes," then, says Jesuit pedagogy, you will experience absolute joy. Put aside the progress managers and the spreadsheets, the testing and the targets, the data and the delivery systems, and we are now at the very core of what calls teachers to teaching, keeps them in it despite the overwhelming pressures and demands of the job, and inspires their students to achieve far beyond levels anyone thought possible.

This is meaningful learning and mindful teaching that goes to the heart of the human condition. It acknowledges our needs for emotional engagement, our quest for excellence, and our craving for relatedness and purpose. There is no proselytizing here: simply a welcoming into important questions that have inspired the greatest thinkers across the ages.

One of us has been working with teacher leader Elizabeth MacDonald and a group of Boston Public School teachers to explore the concept of mindfulness in contemporary education in a project called *The Mindful Teacher*. Over the course of four years, the teachers developed their own "seven synergies of mindful teaching."[40]

1. *Open mindedness.* Especially when learning outcomes are heavily prescribed and students have few opportunities to define their own

goals, openness to students' other strengths and assets is important for building confidence and trust.

2. *Caring and loving.* Struggling students, striving to be more resilient, need to know that their teachers are "on their side," especially when students are taking standardized examinations that don't allow them to show what they know and can do.

3. *Stopping.* The "art of release" contains its own possibilities for learning by reflecting on the rush of events and attending to forms of learning such as artistic expression that find scant realization in a target-driven curriculum.

4. *Professional expertise.* Students and parents are counting on teachers to have the specialized training that will allow them to explore diverse pedagogical strategies with students when conventional approaches prove limited.

5. *Authentic alignment of the teacher's pedagogy with his or her values.* It isn't enough just to have curriculum standards aligned across district and state guidelines if educators themselves find the standards have been hastily assembled, are pedagogically suspect, and are at odds with their core values.

6. *Integration.* The either/or approaches of "flavor-of-the-month" reforms don't allow teachers to develop inclusive repertoires that acknowledge the expertise they have accumulated over time.

7. *Collective responsibility.* The Finnish sense of a broadly shared social obligation to educate the young is both more effective and morally superior to the accountancy measures of the New Orthodoxy that fixate blame on schools in which students' socioeconomic status remains the best predictor of educational outcomes.

What is it that prevents teachers from bringing greater mindful awareness to their classroom practices? Contrary to the opinions of some of our colleagues in research universities, we do not hold that the problem is that we need to know yet more about how students learn effectively. The reality is that the science of learning has made enormous strides in the past 20 years. Brain-based learning, learning styles, and habits of mind all address how to shape learning for children and adults who learn in different ways. Prior knowledge, culturally responsive pedagogy, and problem-based learning highlight how to connect learning to what young people have learned in the past and to what engages them in the present. Metacognition, assessment for learning, and learning how to learn together raise students' awareness of how they learn and enable them to plan and set goals with others.

Nor is the problem one of not knowing how to implement these strategies. Demonstration, training, one-on-one coaching, and finely tuned leadership support have worked in a wide variety of schools across a number of nations. Continuous monitoring through the effective use of data by teachers who know how to blend evidence with creativity and intuition in their teaching has succeeded with even the most traditionally underserved students in the most unlikely settings.[41]

The problem is not lack of knowledge about teaching and learning. It is the distracters in the system that divert teachers from the core purposes and proven practices that support and sustain their capacity to teach well. Mandated targets, endless testing, scripted programs, a tsunami of spreadsheets, profusions of standards, banks of rubrics, and overwhelming emphases on basics—these are the things that drive teachers to distraction.

The distractions do not stop there. They also include the displaced children who interrupt your class midyear because their families are fleeing from debt collectors or from war and conflict overseas, or the "helicopter" parents who constantly hector you to raise their precious children's grades, or the substitute teachers who have unsettled your class while you were undertaking professional development elsewhere, or the dramatic shifts in direction that are repeatedly instigated by yet another principal or superintendent, and then another and another after that!

Despite these unavoidable imperfections and distractions that beset not only teaching but all professions, teachers and school leaders, like the hand-washing physicians described earlier by Atul Gawande, collectively already know most of what needs to be known in order to teach well. We have found outstanding teachers in the most out-of-the-way schools in the most impoverished areas. Where we need help is in identifying and spreading the "positive deviance" that Gawande described, through lateral learning among educators. This is the essence of the idea of professional learning communities, where leaders pull responsible, qualified, and highly capable teachers together in pursuit of improvement within a culture that celebrates persistent questioning and celebration of the art and craft of teaching.

It is time to rediscover, reconnect with, and revivify the heart and soul of what teaching is about—what brings the best people into this great calling and then keeps them there, despite everything. In the Fourth Way, personalized learning will mean infinitely more than customized teaching and learning. It will be mindful learning and teaching that makes us more thoughtful in all senses of the word and therefore more fully human. It will be learning for life.

THREE PRINCIPLES OF PROFESSIONALISM

Teachers are the ultimate arbiters of educational change. The classroom door is the open portal to innovation or the raised drawbridge that holds innovation at bay. No plan for sustainable educational change can ignore or bypass the teacher. School leaders can stand on their heads, dish out awards, or wave pom-poms in the air, but none of it matters unless all teachers are engaged in the changes that have to be achieved.

It's time to insist on more than compliance with or "fidelity" to bureaucratic mandates. It's time to bring teachers back in. The Third Way promoted professional learning communities, but these degenerated into contrived collegiality when the purposes of discussion were confined to increasing achievement scores fixed in advance by policymakers and civil servants in central offices. The Third Way's sponsorship of school networks also increased lateral professional energy, but this was often restricted to fleeting interactions about simple strategies that would give school test scores a quick lift. The Third Way reinvigorated and restored pride among the teaching profession. The Fourth Way pushes this professionalism much farther. Three principles are at the heart of it:

- high-quality teachers,
- positive and powerful professional associations, and
- lively learning communities.

1. HIGH-QUALITY TEACHERS

High-quality learning depends on highly qualified teachers and teaching. Finnish teachers are attracted by their country's inspiring and inclusive vision that accords high status to and strong support for them as builders of their nation's future. It is this principle, not teachers' pay, that makes teaching in Finland highly competitive. Recall that Finnish teachers are paid at the OECD average, just slightly lower than the average of teachers in the United Kingdom and the United States. Here, as elsewhere, the attractions of teacher pay are like those of a long-time romantic partner in which personal appearances remain important but are balanced out by other factors such as intelligence, wit, and charm. Once unattractive pay has been avoided, teachers are drawn by other intrinsic qualities in the work. In Finland, retention is high because conditions are good and teachers feel trusted, so educational leaders don't have to spend countless hours mentoring beginning teachers who then leave the profession after just two or three years.

Finns control teacher quality at the point of entry. They get high-quality teachers and know how to keep them by giving teachers status, support, small classes, and considerable autonomy. Contrast this with U.S. policies that have advocated "tearing down the wall" of teacher certification by making it easy for applicants to circumvent university-based systems for preparing new teachers.[42] U.S. policymakers, it seems, want to *raise* the bar in *learning* by *lowering* the bar in *teaching*!

Of course, there are circumstances where low-cost, flexible routes into teaching are warranted, such as in isolated rural areas or poor urban communities where new teachers can be recruited from within the community without them having to leave it. The U.S. "Grow Your Own" program was started by community organizations in Chicago in collaboration with a local university. Similar programs in Tower Hamlets and elsewhere in the United Kingdom help to strengthen ties between schools and communities by building a stable and locally committed teaching population in the urban areas that most need it. However, short-term, six-week training programs such as those offered by Teach for America in the United States or Teach First in the United Kingdom that attract elite graduates into teaching for two or three years before they move on to other careers are helpful only as emergency, stop-gap measures. The idea is to "teach first," then go elsewhere—the epitome of unsustainable change. We wouldn't want the doctors or dentists who repair our bodies to be trained like this, so why would we want it for those who develop our children's minds?

As in Finland, teacher training needs to be properly accredited at a rigorous practical and intellectual standard that is becoming of a demanding profession. It should start after graduation in a first degree when highly motivated applicants are more sure of their career choice and when the probabilities of subsequent dropout are reduced. This increases quality, reduces training costs, and contributes to stability and sustainability within the system. There are no quick fixes for creating quality teaching such as signing bonuses, performance-based pay, or relabeling qualifications as master's degrees. It is the mission, status, conditions, and rewards of the job, as well as the quality and timing of training, that matter most. This is how we will get and keep the best.

2. POSITIVE AND POWERFUL PROFESSIONAL ASSOCIATIONS

Once a teacher is working in real school settings with all their unanticipated challenges, continuous professional learning and improvement helps retain teachers and further raise the standards of their work. One of the most welcome parts of the Third Way was its renewal of attention to professional standards and recognition. The Second Way of change had sapped professional motivation by mandating prescriptive teaching approaches, but the Third Way began to restore dignity and discretion to the profession once more. One means by which Anglo-American countries have attempted to do this has been by establishing self-regulating bodies of educators—like similar bodies in medicine and law—to register new members, deal with misconduct, promote teacher advocacy, and develop professional teaching standards. However, the distracting paths of autocracy, technocracy, and effervescence have mainly kept real control of teachers' standards in the hands of controlling government bureaucracies, often in the form of narrow criteria of basic competency.

In contrast to these bureaucratic models of professional quality control, self-regulating bodies with robust standards that are upheld and accredited through peer review have been largely peripheral and voluntary. The National Board of Professional Teaching Standards (NBPTS) in the United States, for example, has accredited less than 2% of all of America's public school teachers.[43] Where membership has been compulsory and comprehensive, as in the Ontario College of Teachers (OCT) that one of us helped create in the 1990s, subsequent union influence meant that standards remained general and advisory except for newly qualified teachers and accreditation of training and development programs.[44]

Unions have missed an opportunity to raise professional standards among all their members and increase their credibility and transparency among the public. Government, meanwhile, has kept an iron grip on defining and controlling professional standards. This is professionalism without power—*and teachers know it.*

The Fourth Way will re-create and renew teachers' associations, getting beyond collective bargaining and professional development provision alone, to address the public's desire for a profession that places the well-being of children at the heart of its vocation. Groups such as the Teacher Union Reform Network (TURN) have been in the vanguard of this change, endorsing the highest principles of public service through continual, lifelong learning.[45]

- In the United States, we are advising the California Teachers Association (CTA) on the implementation of the Quality Education Investment Act that repositions this teacher's union as an agent of positive change that benefits student learning and achievement instead of mainly being a defender of its members' interests.
- In Canada, the Alberta Teachers' Association is pressing its provincial government to abandon the government's accountability scheme for a Fourth Way solution that focuses on teacher-developed student assessment within professional standards of practice for which teachers are responsible—using lateral professional energy not to bolster government control, but to engage powerful professional responsibility to raise standards together.

- In New York City, more than one-third of the public schools are networked together as "empowerment schools" where schools and their teachers are granted significantly increased autonomy in exchange for striving to meet agreed standards of achievement.
- In Ontario, the provincial government has given millions of dollars to the Ontario Teachers' Federation with only one condition: that it be spent on staff development to support more positive union involvement in professional development, and to strengthen the culture that deals with this side of the union's work.

In the Fourth Way, Third Way themes of professional recognition and self-regulation are recaptured and redirected through an inspiring and compelling mission that puts teachers' associations at the forefront of change. Robust standards are raised and applied by accredited peers to all members of the profession. Coherent and empowering frameworks of professional learning that embody and advance the standards go beyond courses and workshops to include coaching colleagues, mentoring new teachers, studying new research findings, and writing curriculum materials together.

This is the one place where performance-based pay has promise. It should not be a front-loaded bribe to younger teachers, nor a bonus justified by dubious test score data and sketchy statistics. Rather, teachers can be rewarded for performance based on the following:

- *Multiple indicators*, to get beyond single test scores
- *Performance over cycles of two to three years*, to overcome the dips and blips of unusual events or difficult years
- *Professional service within and beyond their school, validated by a community of peers* who are not confined to immediate associates— to circumvent cronyism and obviate envy

3. LIVELY LEARNING COMMUNITIES

Although teachers can be brilliant innovators, their collective record on sustainable improvement is little better than that of their governments. Decades ago, Dan Lortie noted that the classroom isolation of teachers led them to develop non-innovative cultures of conservatism, individualism, and what he called "presentism"—a fixation on the short term.[46] Excluded from opportunities to engage in long-term planning by their administrators and policymakers, teachers focused on daily challenges and immediate, concrete rewards in their work. Innovations were episodic and fleeting, enjoying little lasting support from leaders or colleagues. In the face of apathy and bureaucracy, teachers withdrew into their classroom cocoons. Standardized reforms of the Second Way made teachers *more* alienated and isolated still.[47]

In response to these pervasive problems, Third Way reformers have promoted more teacher collaboration and inquiry. Collaborative cultures are strongly associated with increased student success and improved retention among new teachers. They provide the mutual learning and moral support that stimulate teachers and sustain them through the difficulties of change. These elements are exhibited in Finland's professional teaching cultures of trust, cooperation, and responsibility, and in the lateral learning networks of sharing across schools within the *RATL* project.

However, collaborative cultures are not always connected to learning and achievement. When they concentrate on planning staff social activities, developing student behavior codes, or swapping test-prep strategies, they become just another distraction from the core tasks of teaching.[48] Even worse, during the Second Way of standardization and the Third Way's New Orthodoxy of performance-driven change, mandated coaching and collaboration have often turned genuine teacher inquiry into rituals of contrived collegiality.[49] Meanwhile, data-driven improvement within what have come to be called Professional Learning Communities, or PLCs, has stapled teachers to their spreadsheets and kept them calculating and concentrating on tested achievement gains, instead of inspiring animated professional discussion about students and their learning.[50]

This should not blind us to the best PLCs, which are not merely an assemblage of teams but living communities and lively cultures dedicated to improving the lifelong learning of students and adults. Teachers in the best PLCs do not just interpret spreadsheets, deliver measurable results, or complete assigned tasks in hastily convened teams. Instead, they are committed to

- transforming the learning that is responsible for results;
- valuing each other as people in relationships of care, respect, and challenge; and
- using quantifiable evidence and shared experience to inquire into teaching and learning issues and make judgments about how to improve them.

In these schools, data *inform* but do not *drive* judgments about practice. All teachers engage in multiple and overlapping learning teams to improve their practice, not just in mandated meetings that are directly connected to test results. Teachers and administrators, and not just the principal or district, define their focus and set targets together. Like Finnish teachers and some of the innovative schools in the *Change Over Time* study, they develop curriculum and define their own educational purposes rather than merely delivering the purposes of others. They teach as well as talk together. As in Tower Hamlets, the PLC includes students, parents, and support staff as well as teachers. Finally, members of the community care about each other as people in long-term relationships as well as about the outcomes of their short-term teams.

In the *Mindful Teacher* project with Boston Public Schools that we described earlier in this chapter, monthly Saturday seminars were established to calm and concentrate teachers' minds in the face of innovation overload and change-related chaos.[51] Using formal meditation practices, teachers were invited to observe the thoughts that preoccupied them in relation to their teaching with empathy and compassion. All kinds of issues emerged—from the classroom management struggles of a novice teacher, to ambivalence about an impending union strike, to the cynical practice of "stacking" students with severe behavioral problems in the class of a beginning teacher who lacked the confidence to stand up to her senior colleagues.

The group then worked on these topics together in an atmosphere of collegiality and support. In twos and threes, they adapted a "tuning protocol" piloted by the Coalition of Essential Schools to guide in-depth discussions on all aspects of their topic for up to two hours. Subsequent meetings then introduced research on teacher-selected topics—examining and engaging with the full range of findings and their implications for teachers.

When teachers have structured opportunities to explore the nitty-gritty challenges of their practice through thoughtful exchanges with colleagues and in relation to relevant research, they rediscover the passion for learning and their own personal and professional growth that brought them into teaching in the first place.

Teachers wrote journals on the meetings and their professional consequences. One experienced teacher decided to ride the school bus with the children every day because violence on and off it had reeled out of control, making learning for the children when they finally arrived at school an impossibility. A beginning elementary teacher found support for his decision to set aside district programs for brief periods each day to ensure he was connecting with the English language learners who had been left behind by the emphasis on test-prep activities. Other teachers learned how policies implemented in their own school that were allegedly mandatory were actually the principal's decision and not mandatory at all. After these meetings, teachers returned to their schools with knowledge, inspiration, and confidence to realign their practices with their moral purposes and beliefs as well as with the available research evidence about children's learning.

In a city where three-quarters of Boston Public Schools' youth had witnessed an act of violence in the previous year, teachers described and discussed the impact of violent incidents on their own students, including their students' ability to learn. Other discussions revolved around alternative approaches to literacy, the kinds of items that appeared on the state's standardized tests, and their schools' prospects for meeting the government targets for Adequate Yearly Progress. Teachers were not in revolt against reforms, but they craved ways to address the genuine concerns behind the targets while remaking their classrooms into environments where children could develop their confidence and skills. And almost incessantly, teachers sought validation that all their hours of hard work, professional training, and care for students were appreciated and worth it.

The *Mindful Teacher* project alerts us to the overlooked ingredients of lively learning communities. While professional learning communities need to address the achievement gap, they must avoid doing this obsessively. PLCs must embody Richard Sennett's "art of release," where the push to improve achievement means learning to let go sometimes.[52] Children's learning cannot be separated from their lives. Deliberations about teachers' pedagogical strategies cannot be disentangled from discussions about these same teachers' emotional engagements with their students and their work. Not all conversations about teaching need to be connected to a test score or a target. Learning communities must be allowed to come alive by enabling students to explore a wide range of questions that can take them in surprising and rewarding directions.

Lively learning communities must be mindful and meaningful learning communities—interested in the children who come to school each day as well as attentive to results. They are places for celebration and commiseration as well as for constructing clear plans. They are informed by statistical evidence and by the wisdom of accumulated experience. Conflict and disagreement are as likely in them as congeniality and consensus; dissonance is what Saul Alinsky called "the music of democracy."[53] PLCs are places to review and renew professional values and not just places to implement government policies and rack up results. The satirical talking fish is as much a part of a lively learning community as any paper plan. In the Fourth Way, professional learning communities develop curriculum and don't just deliver it. They set ambitious targets together rather than running a furious and frantic race to meet the targets imposed by others.

FOUR CATALYSTS OF COHERENCE

The hardest part of educational change is not how to start it, but how to make it last and spread. Pilot projects almost always show early promise, but most attempts to scale them up produce pale imitations of the original. There will always be a few exceptional schools, but we need many more of them. Permissive, voluntary networks work mainly with volunteers and enthusiasts and rarely reach the rest. And leaders of quick turnarounds seldom stay around to see them through. The challenge of coherence is not to clone or align everything so it looks the same in all schools. If we are all on the same page, nobody is reading the entire book! The challenge, rather, is how to bring diverse people together to work skillfully and effectively for a common cause that lifts them up and has them moving in the same direction with an impact on learning, achievement, and results. The Fourth Way has four catalysts that create this coherence:

- sustainable leadership,
- integrating networks,
- responsibility before accountability, and
- differentiation and diversity.

1. SUSTAINABLE LEADERSHIP

Leadership is the afterthought of educational change. It's the cigarette that's smoked after the reform has been consummated—or at least, that's how it often seems. Systemwide reform efforts typically pull leaders together for one or two meetings, then just hope they will follow through on their own. Alternatively, governments bypass leadership altogether and go straight to the classroom through teacher-proof and leader-proof programs of prescribed delivery. For example, almost 50% of Florida's Educational Leadership Examination, essential for principal certification, addresses knowledge of and compliance with state legislation.[54] These emphases and others like them pay little or no attention to leaders who might wish to develop the people's capacity to lead changes of their own. Principals in these systems are not being trained to be leaders, but rather to be compliant line managers. They are granted increased responsibility but diminished autonomy.

It is rare to have an explicit strategy of leadership development that connects it directly to strategies of educational reform, yet change without leadership has no chance of being sustainable. The leadership agenda is the change agenda. They are one and the same. The reform environment has to create conditions where leaders do not merely implement external mandates, but have the capacity and flexibility to make changes themselves.

In the Third Way of educational change, leadership finally received attention after its abandonment or conversion into mere management during the Second Way. This shift has been precipitated by

- a "perfect storm" that consists of a massive retirement of the Baby Boomer generation of leadership with few successors immediately behind it;

- a different generational mission in the younger cohort of incoming potential leaders that includes more women and is more concerned about work-life balance; and
- a reform environment that makes existing school leaders so overloaded and vulnerable that their Number 2s are reluctant to take on the job.[55]

Responses to this succession crisis have taken the form of aspiring and emerging leadership programs to identify talent early, provide mentoring and coaching, and construct clear routes up ascending escalators and along lateral walkways of leadership opportunities. Yet these initiatives deal only with the supply side of leadership, with increasing the flow of leaders along the leadership pipeline.

By contrast, Tom Hatch points out that leadership capacity has similarities to water capacity. It must be developed by reducing unnecessary demand as well as by increasing supply.[56] The leaders in the *RATL* network learned that abandonment is part of the armament of leading for change. Leaders can't do everything. When leadership turns into management of innumerable imposed initiatives and being evaluated according to unfair and inappropriate forms of accountability, it's not surprising that no one wants to lead anymore.

So what can be done strategically when the demand is unappealing and the supply is scarce? One of the most promising answers is *distributed leadership*. Distributed leadership creates pools among classroom teachers from which future higher-level leaders come. It entails developing leadership early among many, and not just among the chosen few who show obvious potential.[57]

School leaders in high-performing Finland practice distributed leadership. They are part of the "society of experts" in their schools. Their collective responsibility supersedes the line-management of administrative accountability. And when teachers exercise collective responsibility for all students, they also prepare for promotion to principal in their own schools—ensuring that shared leadership also supports effective and sustainable leadership succession.

Distributed leadership draws change *from* the everyday knowledge and capacities of staff rather than driving reforms *through* them. Like community organizers, skilled educational leaders have to build social capital and leadership from the human resources already around them, taking a second look at the assets possessed by their staff that have not yet been mobilized and acted on. The director of Tower Hamlets established ambitious achievement targets *with* her team of head teachers over and above the targets that government imposed *on* them. The *RATL* project has distributed leadership throughout its entire network that now numbers more than 700 schools, where leaders working with leaders has become a key driver of change.

Distributed leadership does *not* mean voting on everything, giving way to groupthink, or having the majority always decide. These misconceptions recall Oscar Wilde's quip that socialism requires too many meetings! Rather, principals of the most innovative schools that practiced distributed leadership in the *Change Over Time* project acknowledged that, while most of their decisions were collaborative, many were primarily consultative and—under pressures of time or confidentiality—some were even individual and almost arbitrary. But when these less collaborative moments arose, principals made decisions with their staff's trust and consent that, to the best of their ability, they would act in everyone's best interests, in relation to the community's agreed purposes.

Distributed leadership is a crucial element of what one of us has defined as *sustainable* leadership. Distributed leadership is grounded in and advances a compelling and inclusive moral purpose. It is a shared responsibility, which benefits future generations, uses resources wisely, and does no harm to others in the surrounding environment. Beyond the revolving doors of leadership that plague many systems today, sustainable leadership builds capacity and develops leadership succession in a dynamic and integrated strategy of change. The seven principles of sustainable leadership are a fundamental part of the Fourth Way.[58]

1. *Depth*—of purpose in developing student learning that is challenging and relevant, that is not distorted or overly driven by test data, and that includes attending to issues of environmental sustainability in the curriculum, the community, and the school

2. *Breadth*—so this purpose and its achievement are a shared and distributed responsibility, not an heroic exception or an isolated indulgence

3. *Endurance*—over time so that improvement continues across reforms and beyond particular governments, carrying over from one leader to the next through effectively managed succession where school improvement plans include succession plans and everyone prepares for his or her own obsolescence

4. *Justice*—in attending to all students' learning and achievement, narrowing the gaps between the most- and least-advantaged of them, and promoting cooperation rather than ruthless competition among stronger schools and their weaker neighbors

5. *Resourcefulness*—in using financial resources and human energy at a pace that people can manage, rather than wastefully burning them out

6. *Conservation*—in connecting future visions to past traditions in narratives of commitment and hope, as in Finland's investment

in creativity or in community organizers' respect for indigenous, local knowledge

7. *Diversity*—of curriculum, pedagogy, and team contributions in organizations and networks where ideas are cross-pollinated instead of being cloned

One promising and productive way for schools and their leaders to assist other schools is represented in the unique *National Leaders of Education* program, introduced in 2006 by England's National College for School Leadership. Here, a national group of outstanding head teachers (or principals) who have demonstrated evidence of success in assisting other schools work closely with struggling partners who approach them to improve learning and results. These leaders do not take over the struggling schools, nor do they send in a team with checklists and quick hit-and-run tactics, nor do they merely offer advice as to how the struggling school should try to improve. Instead, the head teacher and a team of highly trained support staff roll up their sleeves and work with and alongside the school's teachers and administrators to make improvements together. As the existing staff build capacity and the school shows signs of turning around, the *National Leaders* and their teams gradually withdraw. Significant achievement gains have been recorded in the many schools that have participated, and the program is expanding rapidly to meet rising demand in the schools.

In terms of sustainable leadership, the National College for School Leadership program uses leadership systemically so that stronger leaders and leadership teams can help struggling peers. This is leadership for social justice. It provides significant career development for existing school leaders without them having to move away from the world of schools, and it develops capacity and lines of succession within the schools. For leaders to be away from their existing schools while they are assisting others, they also have to be effective in distributing and developing leadership capacity so their schools can continue without them and other leaders can come forward in their stead.

This approach to developing leadership capacity increases the supply side of the leadership pipeline strategically and systemically through leadership practice rather than by mounting leadership preparation programs.[59] It connects leadership to change by developing leaders as agents of change through supporting others, instead of by delivering changes demanded by others. Furthermore, it injects compensatory resources into the helping schools so the assistance their leaders offer does not improve others' capacity at the expense of their own.

Leadership is always important. At great social turning points, it is more important than ever. At times like these, the leadership we need is not leadership that turns us against others or holds us back in awe. It is leadership that lifts us up and turns us around together in pursuit of a common cause that expresses and advances our humanity.

Our schools are the social embryos of humanity—those institutions that we establish to promote our highest collective values. They should be the embodiment of norms of reciprocity, active trust, and democratic deliberation. It is not more mandates and management they need, but the broad shoulders of uplifting and sustainable leadership.

2. INTEGRATING NETWORKS

In most change efforts, improvement is unequal and change fails to spread. Teachers and schools learn best not by reading research reports, listening to speeches, or attending workshops, but by watching, listening to, and learning from each other in the very act of teaching itself. When making change, it is as important to build new relationships among people engaged in practice together as it is to spread new knowledge to them.

One way to disseminate knowledge through relationships is via networks. In natural and social systems, the most effective networks combine properties of emergence (the innovations that arise in open systems through spontaneous and unpredictable cross-pollination and interactions) with the properties of design (shaping the interactions so that cross-breeding moves in a desired direction).[60]

If there is too much emergence and the system is too loose, networks become diffuse and they dissipate. Purposes are unclear. Talk does not turn into action. There is no proof of impact in products, practices, or results. Or networks attract only volunteers and enthusiasts, dividing those who are inside the net from those outside it.[61]

If there is too much design and the system is too tight, networks turn into administratively constructed clusters of schools whose purpose is to implement or serve as a reference group for government policy. In the end, emerging ideas and innovations are suppressed when they conflict with mandated policies or are highjacked by those policies to advance other people's ends. Attempts to control networks ultimately kill them.[62] Governments cannot control networks, nor should they even mandate that every school belong to one. They can only disturb networks by throwing things in for them to deal with.

- The *RATL* network of secondary schools plus the mentor schools with which they are partnered balances emergence with design by providing carefully assembled menus of change strategies for participants to observe and exchange.

- The *Alberta Initiative for School Improvement* that we have recently studied, has large numbers of interconnected schools design their own improvements linked to shared targets and measurable gains in student achievement.
- In Rhode Island and Chicago, the *School Accountability for Learning and Teaching* (*SALT*) project engages schools in developing self-evaluations, which then are connected to external evaluations administered by teams of peers drawn from other schools. This improves capacity not only in the host schools but also in the teams that evaluate them.

In all these cases, educators have a clear, common, and urgent purpose linked to learning, achievement, and improvement. Participation is invited rather than being compulsory or permissive. Governments or foundations *initiate* and *fund* (but they do not *interfere* in) the networks so schools do not have to find their own resources and additional time. Experiential knowledge is circulated among respected practitioners, but these interactions are also invigorated and disturbed by the infusion of external ideas and expertise. The result is significant measurable improvement.

Even these best-case scenarios, though, pose two challenges. First, the unrelenting political emphasis on short-term system achievement targets in basic subjects can plunge networks into the effervescent cultures of "presentism" we described earlier. These circulate only short-term solutions and avoid undertaking more laborious, longer-term efforts to transform teaching and learning. The "Nanny state" of constant surveillance and endless intervention is incompatible with the innovation of the net.

Second, continuing competition among high schools, especially, means that networks, federations, and partnerships often work best at a distance among schools that are not in direct competition for clients, or among schools serving younger children where competition is less cut-throat.[63] Schools in the "diverse provider models" that are spreading in the United States have no incentive to give away resources or disclose ideas or expertise that might assist struggling neighbors who are also their immediate competitors.

One of the greatest benefits of school networks is stronger schools that help weaker peers in similar demographic circumstances—in the statistical neighborhoods that are now identifiable through sophisticated and contextualized data in systems such as those in England and Ontario. But the greatest challenges of social justice are often among schools in physically contiguous neighborhoods of the same town or city. Divided by district boundaries that reflect class-based or race-related residential patterns, opposed by the ruthless competition of the market, and isolated by the fear of betraying secrets to the enemy, schools in the same town or city are often the hardest to network.[64]

Yet even these kinds of competition can be overcome. Finnish school leaders share resources and support each other through a sense of common purpose and shared responsibility for all the young people in their town or city. In the more competitive system of England, schools in Tower Hamlets overcame their isolation to support one of their own schools when it started to struggle. At their zenith, the Alliance Schools in Texas also created a shared sense of common purpose when community organizers convened vertical and horizontal meetings of educators in the same regional clusters of schools to share knowledge and develop cross-school strategies.

There are many ways to use educational networks to improve schools and districts. Some of the most important include these:

- Networking and partnerships may start best at a distance and then move closer to home once the benefits of collaborative habits have been established.
- The mayors of towns and cities can exercise inspirational leadership in bringing schools together to pursue a common mission, despite their differences.
- Since inequities between districts are often much greater than within them, national and state governments can target increased funding to schools prepared to advance the interests of social justice by collaborating with less-favored schools across their immediate boundaries.
- As in some English local authorities, high school students might work in their home schools in the morning or on some days, and then mix with other students from other races and cultures across their local network of schools to undertake inspiring and enjoyable learning together on other days or in the afternoons.

In the end, the point of networks is to spread innovation, stimulate learning, increase professional motivation, and reduce inequities. It is to see managed diversity as an integrating strength, and not a dissipating weakness. Networks are a fundamental and not merely fashionable part of the Fourth Way.

3. RESPONSIBILITY BEFORE ACCOUNTABILITY

Responsibility precedes and supersedes accountability. Socrates died because he believed it was his responsibility to teach his students to think for themselves. Confucius insisted that educators had an incontrovertible responsibility to ensure their students were true scholars who modeled a methodical social etiquette that reflected celestial harmony in all their interactions with rich and poor alike. Accountability is the remainder that is left when this responsibility has been subtracted.

- The Finns are held together by cultures of trust, cooperation, and responsibility. They feel responsible for all the children they affect, not just those in their own classes. They lift every child up from the bottom, one at a time. Small classes and generous support for students with special educational needs create a low-key reform climate where teachers can concentrate on individual children, rather than dealing with spreadsheets or responding to bureaucratic interventions.
- Teachers and leaders in the *RATL* network operate in highly transparent systems of lateral engagement that place automatic pressure on them to act responsibly in finding and trying solutions that will help their students succeed.
- Involving large numbers of community members in the schools of Tower Hamlets and in the extended service schools in other parts of the United Kingdom and the United States creates a climate where professionals, parents, and community members rely more on trusted, close relationships than on league tables and test scores as a guide to the effectiveness of their schools.

Test scores and other student assessments are the most commonly used instruments of educational accountability. Although we have been critical of exclusive reliance on test scores as benchmarks of student learning, there is sometimes a place for them. At this time, Finland has no standardized, high-stakes testing. Even in Finland, though, as the country accepts more immigration and ethnic diversity to provide a stronger tax base for its growing number of retirees, teachers may no longer find it easy to understand and intervene with students who do not intuitively look and act like them. Other, more objective data that can be acquired through random sampling of students to be tested may add insight and prod the consciences of teachers who otherwise feel they are doing their best. Despite being top-rated in the world, Finland may therefore need to consider a stronger role for educational testing in the future.

Test and examination data are often collected through a census applied to all schools and children. This occurs when all young people take an examination in order to have a chance of being selected. It also can be helpful for a school to collect comprehensive though confidential data about itself or with trusted peers, so it can work out where and how to improve. However, when high-stakes events such as graduation depend on single or simple measures of performance that are linked to political targets, are cause for possible sanction, and are made public, the chance that they will distort the learning process and lead to widespread corruption is high.[65] Driven to take extra unnecessary steps in order to meet arbitrary performance standards, teachers and leaders feel forced into cheating the system—just like the soccer players who were made to carry electronic chips in their shoes to count their steps.

Fortunately, it is not necessary to ensure accountability through a census. It can be achieved more easily and more effectively through a statistically valid sample. The National Assessment of Educational Progress test in the United States is just such a device.[66] Interestingly, it has shown no significant achievement gains in recent years (with the single exception of fourth-grade mathematics) while statewide tests applied through a census, for which students can be specifically prepared, have risen year after year. From Scotland to Finland, from New Zealand to the islands of Papua New Guinea, accountability is already often achieved by samples. For accountability purposes, test samples are not merely substitutes for a census: they are superior. Most industries exercise quality control by testing samples. It's a waste of money to test everything! Even environmentalists check air quality and pollution levels by samples. This is enough to hold corporations accountable and should be adequate for educators, too.

Yet a shrinking number of governments hang on to accountability by census, even though it is subject to widespread abuse. They do it even though it is exorbitantly expensive—diverting scarce resources from teaching and learning needs elsewhere. And they retain it even despite parents' objections.

However, as we reported in the Preface, in the UK and the Canadian provinces of Alberta and Nova Scotia, systemwide standardized testing by census is firmly in retreat because it's just "not worth it" in terms of the return on the investment. Governments that retain and promote testing by census will increasingly find that they are no longer in the vanguard of school reform, but are bringing up the rear.

A theory-in-action of educational change that is professional, democratic, and sustainable will primarily support those forms of assessment that promote learning in schools. Assessment-for-learning uses a range of diagnostic tests and other assessments that give teachers feedback on individual student problems and progress so they can intervene accordingly and help students manage their own progress. It is an integral part of the process of personalization.[67] Systemwide accountability, meanwhile, can be achieved through prudent sampling rather than through a profligate and politically controlling census. The Fourth Way treats accountability as the conscience or superego of the system that checks it, not as the ego or id that drives it.

4. DIFFERENTIATION AND DIVERSITY

Students are diverse. Organizations are diverse. Change itself is diverse. None of them operates in standardized ways, and they rarely respond well to standardized strategies of improvement.

Standardization and alignment were a response to the inconsistencies in quality that existed under the First Way. But inconsistency is not the same as diversity. Inconsistency is about differences of standard between what's better and what's worse. Diversity is about variable expressions of a standard or even of what counts as a standard. The flaw of the Second Way of standardization is that by attacking inconsistency in areas of basic competency in literacy or mathematics, it also ignored or eradicated diversity—in students, schools, and improvement strategies.

When the curriculum is standardized in detail and tested to excess, it either becomes lopsided and ignores the knowledge and interests of many cultural groups, or it becomes overloaded in trying to address the cultural interests of everyone. Allison Skerrett has looked at the educational policies and school practices of English teaching in the Canadian provinces of Ontario and British Columbia on the one hand and the U.S. states of Massachusetts and Texas on the other.[68] Canada is an officially bilingual and multicultural society that articulates its approach to racial and cultural diversity through a myth of a complex, interlocking mosaic. The United States expresses its approach to immigration and diversity in terms of a contrasting myth of the melting pot. Yet the secondary school English curriculum policies that Skerrett looked at in both countries were equally as exclusionary. Especially as students approached the point of selection for university, recommended and selected texts in both countries became predominantly Anglo-American (and more occasionally European) in character.

Many teachers in both contexts worked hard to address the cultural diversity of their classrooms and communities despite the curriculum constraints. This was particularly true of teachers who had undergone recent professional preparation that addressed issues of diversity effectively, younger teachers who were encountering more diversity in their everyday lives, or teachers who had personally experienced inequalities at some earlier point and who wanted to rectify injustices among others. These teachers worked around and beyond the prescribed curriculum. The scope they had to do this increased as they taught farther away from the courses that regulated university entrance—for example, with younger, special education, or second language students; or with students in lower tracks. But after innovative efforts in the 1980s and early 1990s to promote multiculturalism and even antiracism in schools, both countries eventually succumbed to the Second Way's pressures of standardization and high-stakes testing.

This led to what Skerrett calls a *monocultural restoration* in which standardized content is now geared towards raising performance and meeting targets in statewide or provincewide tests. These reforms have made responding to cultural differences considerably harder.

Linda Nathan, principal of the outstanding Boston Arts Academy, knows this as much as anyone. Although there has been a 15-year rise in scores on the statewide test known as the Massachusetts Comprehensive Assessment System (MCAS), the dropout rate among poor, black, and Latino students has escalated, as a test-centered curriculum of memorizable content that crowds out other more interesting areas of learning speaks less and less to them. With the impact of MCAS, she says,

> [o]ur curriculum has become narrower and less engaging. . . . Our school has had to sacrifice breadth in science teaching. We spent seven years developing a rigorous, engaging curriculum that combined physical and biological sciences and increased in complexity each year. As a result of MCAS testing, we have had to return to a "layer-cake approach," teaching first physical science . . . then chemistry, then biology, all to ensure that students pass the state tests.[69]

When MCAS adds history to the list of subjects tested in Massachusetts, Nathan fears that her teachers will be forced to jettison the outstanding and culturally responsive humanities curriculum they have carefully designed and honed over many years. This includes topics that urban students want to understand and come to terms with through debates about the civil rights movement, position papers on the rise of the Black Panthers, and oral history research on desegregation and school busing in Boston in the 1970s. Of course, this is just the kind of content that stimulates cross-racial conversations and leads to enriched interactions with and learning from their parents and other members of their community. But with the monocultural restoration that is MCAS, these kinds of conversations will be gone. Animated interactions about culturally engaging material will be replaced with and reduced to anal-retentive obsessions with narrowing technical achievement gaps in conventionally tested material.

A school located in the center of England's race riots in 2002 raised achievement by tilting its curriculum towards the visual arts in which its Bangladeshi students excelled. But its outstanding success was then undermined by the government's subsequent announcement of a new squadron of 638 failing schools that included this one. This school, like some of its new peers, had secured high percentages of students achieving the critical minimum standard of five Grades C and above in the General Certificate of Secondary Education (GCSE) examination. Nevertheless, these failed to include the government's changed requirement for conventional mathematics and English to be included in these passes.[70]

With one swish of the technocrat's pen, this turned-around school was no longer *feted*, but *failing*—part of a newly defined cohort that would get the public's attention and attract the political sanction of yet more government intervention and surveillance. The outstanding achievements in visual arts through which Bangladeshi students had been acquiring much of their literacy would now have to be replaced by mandated study of the traditional and often exclusionary canon.

The world is becoming more, not less, diverse, global, and interconnected. A restricted, standardized diet of curriculum basics fails to connect with or capitalize on this diversity. It tries to raise expectations, push harder, and have everyone be more diligent with curriculum materials and test preparations—but these engage fewer and fewer of our students. We are raising the bar in tested standardization, while high numbers of poor and minority dropouts are falling through the cracks beneath us.

The Fourth Way is better suited to dealing with diversity among our students by

- developing an inclusive and uplifting purpose that inspires them and all who work with them;
- engaging with and learning from their communities;
- attracting high-quality teachers who have been trained to understand and work well with diversity;
- ensuring that the supporting conditions and salaries for teachers and leaders working in conditions of high poverty and great diversity at least match and sometimes outstrip those to be found in more affluent and monocultural suburbs;
- developing curriculum locally within frameworks that allow appropriate cultural responsiveness, while having to address clear yet broad standards in which teachers' curricula and pedagogy must consistently address and respond to the diversity in their schools and society;
- creating incentives, expectations, and structural supports so that strong schools can assist and learn from weaker partners, not only within districts but also across them;
- abandoning the restrictive obsession with tested standardization that began in the Second Way and has persisted into the Third Way; and
- engaging with, though never automatically endorsing, all the diversities of our students and societies, including those that define the dominant culture, for it is mutual empathy and animated engagement, not mere tolerance, uncritical celebration, and passive endorsement, that are the secrets of successful diversity.

This challenge of diversity cannot be denied or delimited by the antiseptic approach of narrowing arithmetical achievement gaps. It is one that must engage us all directly. Have one-on-one meetings with students' parents, venturing out into the community rather than simply waiting for parents to come to school. Study your students' home cultures by inviting parents and other community members to come to class as guest speakers on topics of interest. Reflect on where diversity appears in your life as well as your work. Who do you have round for dinner? Who are your children's friends? Who do they date?

Push beyond cardboard celebrations of diversity to help students see that every culture is enlivened by debates about what to retain from the past and what to give up for the future. If you work in a monocultural community, this is where attention to diversity through overseas visits to developing countries, international networks of connection to more diverse schools, partnerships with poorer schools and districts, and an outward, cosmopolitan engagement with a culturally diverse and global curriculum matter most of all.

CONCLUSION

The Fourth Way is neither about letting a thousand flowers bloom nor about micromanaging everything in detail. It neither exalts the market and its charter school prodigies nor extols the virtues of an all-providing state. In this sense, the Fourth Way shares important commonalities with its Third Way predecessor (Figure 4.2).

Acknowledging these important areas of overlap and continuity, the Fourth Way is nevertheless a clear departure from Third Way thinking in all other respects. It is not a way to retain autocratic control over narrowly defined goals and targets. The Fourth Way, rather, is a democratic and pro-fessional path to improvement that builds from the bottom, steers from the top, and provides support and pressure from the sides. Through high-quality teachers committed to and capable of creating deep and broad teaching and learning, it builds powerful, responsible, and lively profes-sional communities in an increasingly self-regulating but not self-absorbed or self-seeking profession. Here, teachers define and pursue high stan-dards and shared targets, and improve by learning continuously through networks, from evidence, and from each other.

In the Fourth Way, a resilient social democracy builds an inspiring and inclusive vision through courageous national and state or provincial lead-ership that draws teachers to the profession and grants them public status within it. It involves parents and the public as highly engaged partners, along with businesses that show corporate educational responsibility. In

Figure 4.2   Third and Fourth Way Commonalities

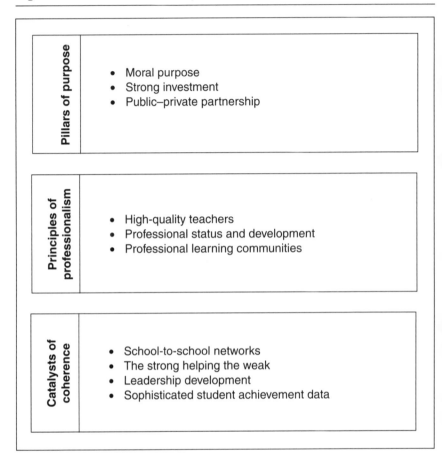

the Fourth Way, a lot is expected of educators, but the burden of narrowing achievement gaps and achieving social justice does not rest on their shoulders alone. It is shared with a strongly supported health service, housing system, and social service sector.

In all this, students in the Fourth Way are not merely targets of change. They are vigorous and active partners with a leading voice in their own development. This partnership is neither paternalistic nor indulgent but calls for educators who demand high standards, do not accept weak excuses or shabby work, and provide the consistent pressure and strong support to raise students to the highest levels of achievement.

The Fourth Way achieves coherence by

- developing sustainable leadership that is knowledgeable about learning;

- placing responsibility before accountability (with accountability serving as a conscience through sampling);
- initiating and supporting but not overregulating professional networks of improvement;
- conducting an assault on the excesses of tested standardization that deny diversity and destroy creativity; and—most of all—
- developing an inspiring and inclusive educational and social vision that connects the future to the past and leaves teachers collectively responsible for pedagogical decisions and a good amount of curriculum development within it.

The three converging yet somewhat slippery paths of the autocracy, the technocracy, and effervescence that made up the New Orthodoxy beyond the Third Way were ultimately only about deliverology. The Fourth Way promotes educational change through deepened and demanding learning, professional quality and engagement, and invigorated community development and public democracy. Remember: The Fourth Way shares important commonalities with the Third (as well as legacies from the Ways before that), but it is a significant shift from, and even disruption of, Third Way orthodoxy. These shifts and disruptions are represented in Figure 4.3.

We are at a turning point in history. The Old Ways can no longer serve us, and some of them have even actively betrayed us. We are in an increasingly interconnected world, financially, politically, and culturally. Unrestrained markets have held us hostage to caprice and greed. Standardization has undermined our capacity to understand and deal with diversity. We will need more innovation and creativity in the 21st century, not less. We will need more connection to and interdependence with our neighbors, at home and abroad, rather than an arrogant insistence on operating alone. It is time to reshape the world and to reinvent ourselves within it. This is the call of the Fourth Way.

We have caught glimpses of the Fourth Way in the nation of Finland, in the network that is *RATL*, and in the community organizing and development work of Tower Hamlets and many American cities.

We offer no silver bullets and make no promises. There are many tensions in the Fourth Way that will require sound judgment, not simple solutions. The Fourth Way places new demands on teachers *and* students, on top-ranking policymakers *and* bottom-up community organizers. Lateral pressures *and* supports will bring discomfort to some and energize and inspire others. We will need to attend to and integrate both short-term *and* long-term considerations, and sacrifice neither to the other. We must find ways to help our school neighbors in ways that also energize and empower ourselves. At a crucial turning point in global history, we have to make daring and disruptive changes, not incremental adjustments—but

Figure 4.3   Third Way New Orthodoxy to Fourth Way Solutions

		Third Way New Orthodoxy	Fourth Way Solutions
		from ⟶	*to*
Pillars of Purpose and Partnership	Change	Detailed deliverology	Steering and development
	Control	Bureaucratic, market-related, and professional	Democratic and professional
	Trust	Public confidence	Active trust
	Goals	Competitive, measurable standards	Inspiring, innovative, and inclusive mission
	Public	Parent choice and community service delivery	Public engagement and community development
	Partnership	Entrepreneurial and expedient	Transparent and responsible
	Learning	Customized learning	Mindful learning and teaching
	Students	Targets of teaching and service delivery	Engagement and voice
Principles of Professionalism	Teacher quality	Reward- and performance-driven	Mission- and conditions-driven
	Teacher associations	Bought-off distracters, who consent to change	Agents of change
	Professional community	Data-driven	Evidence-informed
Catalysts of Coherence	Quality assurance	Accountability first	Responsibility first
	Accountability	By census	By sample
	Targets	Arbitrary and imposed	Ambitious and shared
	Leadership	Individually developed	Systemic and sustainable
	Lateral relations	Dispersed networks	Networks plus area-based collaboration
	Diversity and social Justice	Narrowed achievement gaps and data-driven interventions	Demanding and responsive teaching

without abandoning everything we have valued and achieved in the past. And moment by moment, one issue at time, we have to learn how to steer clearly from the top while knowing how and when to "let go."

In the Fourth Way, there will be standards, including public, human, business, and ethical ones, but there will no longer be educational standardization. There will also be targets, and these will be even bolder because dedicated professionals will identify them together. There will be hard work and persistence, but not pointless drudgery. There will be greater support for the education profession, but not unconditionally. Accountability will be our conscience, not our Grand Inquisitor. And our children will be the deposits of learning, generosity, and humanity through which we invest in the future.

The purpose of the Fourth Way is to create the schools that will undergird and catalyze our best values to regenerate and improve society. The time is surely nigh for this. New generations are taking over. The age of unregulated markets and wanton greed is disappearing behind us. People are starting to look within and beyond themselves once more. Now is the time to join them.

We must be clear where we stand as we face one of the most critical turning points of all time. We must stand aside from the slippery and distracting paths of easy opportunism that merely enhance government "deliverology." We must take the more vertiginous route that scales the heights of professional excellence and public democracy. For it is this truly challenging path that will lead us to the peaks of excellence and integrity in student learning and its resulting high levels of achievement.

Taking the familiar well-traveled path is easy, even when it does not benefit children or their communities. It is time to step up and step out in order to reach a higher purpose and a better place. In this sense, the classic lines of Robert Frost that urge us to take an unfamiliar route can be viewed not just as an incitement to individualism, but as an inspiration for collective courage and initiative:

> I shall be telling this with a sigh
> Somewhere ages and ages hence:
> Two roads diverged in a wood, and I—
> I took the one less traveled by,
> And that has made all the difference.[71]

ENDNOTES

———— ■■ ————

PREFACE

1. El-Erian, M. A. (2008). *When markets collide: Investment strategies for the age of global economic change.* New York: McGraw Hill.

2. Raney, A., Heeter, C. (Producers), Heeter, C. (Director/Editor), & Raney, A. (Writer). (2007). *Two million minutes* [Motion picture]. Indianapolis, IN: Broken Pencil.

3. Farley, J. (2006, March 12). Improving math ed—Bush right about that— But where are the teachers coming from? *San Francisco Chronicle.* Retrieved on November 23, 2008, from http://www.sfgate.com; Kristof, N. (2004, February 11). Watching the jobs go by. *New York Times.* Retrieved November 24, 2008, from http://www.nytimes.com

4. New Commission on the Skills of the American Workforce. (2007). *Tough choices or tough times: The report of the new commission on the skills of the American workforce.* Washington, DC: National Center on Education and the Economy.

5. The results of this research are reported in Hargreaves, A., & Goodson, I. (2006). Educational change over time? Special issue of *Educational Administration Quarterly, 42*(1); Hargreaves, A., & Fink, D. (2006). *Sustainable leadership.* San Francisco: Jossey-Bass; Hargreaves, A. (2003). *Teaching in the knowledge society: Education in the age of insecurity.* New York: Teachers College Press and Maidenhead, UK: Open University Press.

6. The initial research evaluation of this project is reported in Hargreaves, A., Shirley, D., Evans, M., Johnson, C., & Riseman, D. (2007). *The long and short of school improvement: Final evaluation of the Raising Achievement, Transforming Learning Programme of the Specialist Schools and Academies Trust.* London: Specialist Schools and Academies Trust.

7. See Hargreaves, A., Halász, G., & Pont, B. (2008). The Finnish approach to system leadership. In Pont, B., Nusche, D., & Hopkins, D. (Eds.), *Improving school leadership, Vol. 2: Case studies on system leadership* (pp. 69–109). Paris: OECD.

8. Some of this work is contained in Orr, M., & Rogers, J. (Eds.). (Forthcoming). *Public engagement for public education.* Palo Alto, CA: Stanford University Press.

9. See MacDonald, E., & Shirley, D. (2009). *The mindful teacher.* New York: Teachers College Press.

CHAPTER 1

1. The NCLB quote is cited in Hoff, D. (2007). "Growth models" gaining in accountability debate. *Education Week, 27*(16), 22–25. The survey results of educators can be found in Public Agenda. (2006). Reality check 2006: Issue no 3: Is support for standards and testing fading? New York: Author. The high profile commission is the New Commission on the Skills of the American Workforce. See National Center on Education and the Economy (2007). *Tough choices or tough times: The report of the new commission on the skills of the American workforce.* Washington, DC: Author.

2. European Commission, declared March 31, 2008, retrieved from http:// europa.eu/rapid/pressReleasesAction.do?reference=IP/08/482

3. See, for example Aho, E., Pitkänen, K., & Sahlberg, P. (2006). *Policy development and reform principles of basic and secondary education in Finland since 1968.* Washington, DC: World Bank; Hargreaves, A., Halász, G., & Pont, B. (2008). The Finnish approach to system leadership. In B. Pont, D. Nusche, & D. Hopkins (Eds.). (2008). *Improving school leadership, Vol. 2: Case studies on system leadership.* Paris: OECD, 69–109.

4. On objectives and testing, see Shaw, M. (2004, April 9). End testing of infants: Seven is too young for tests say parents in TES poll. *London Times Educational Supplement,* p. 1; Mansell, W., & White, P. (2004, November 12). Stop test drilling, primaries warned. *London Times Educational Supplement,* p. 1. Retrieved from https://www.tes.co.uk/article.aspx?storycode=2047875. The announcement of the end of standardized testing following scandals of incompetence in the testing agency to which the key stage tests at age 14 were contracted out was reported by the BBC in "Tests scrapped for 14-year-olds." Retrieved from http://news.bbc.co.uk/2/hi/uk_news/education/7669254.stm

5. Blair, T., & Schröder, G. (1999). *Europe: The Third Way—die neue mitte.* London: Labor Party and SPD.

6. Giddens, A. (1999). *The Third Way: The renewal of social democracy.* Malden, MA: Blackwell; Giddens, A. (2000). *The Third Way and its critics.* Cambridge, UK: Polity Press; Giddens, A. (Ed.). (2001). *The global Third Way debate.* Cambridge, UK: Polity Press.

7. Lowenthal, D. (1986). *The past is a foreign country.* Cambridge: Cambridge University Press. The phrase was first used by Leslie Poles Hartley, (1953/2002). *The go-between.* New York: NYRB Classics, p. 17.

8. Giddens, *The Third Way*; Giddens, *The global Third Way debate.*

9. Kohl, H. (1967). *36 children.* New York: New American Library; Kozol, J. (1967). *Death at an early age: The destruction of the hearts and mind of Negro children in the Boston Public Schools.* Boston: Houghton Mifflin Company.

10. Hargreaves, A., & Goodson, I. (2006). Educational change over time? The sustainability and non-sustainability of three decades of secondary school

change and continuity. *Educational Administration Quarterly, 42*(1), 3–41. The data and findings that are reported in this chapter are related to the first two Ways of change and the interregnum between them and can be found in more detail in this journal article and in Hargreaves, A., & Fink, D. (2006). *Sustainable leadership.* San Francisco: Jossey-Bass; Hargreaves, A. (2003). *Teaching in the knowledge society: Education in the age of insecurity.* New York: Teachers College Press and Maidenhead, UK: Open University Press. Goodson, I. (2003). *Professional knowledge, professional lives.* Maidenhead, UK: Open University Press.

11. Her Majesty's Inspectorate. (1983). *Curriculum 11–16: Towards a statement of entitlement.* London: HMSO, p. 16.

12. National Commission on Excellence in Education. (1983). *A nation at risk: The imperative for educational reform.* Washington, DC: U.S. Government Printing Office.

13. One of us was involved in producing the review of international literature that provided a foundation for this provincial policy. See Hargreaves, A., Earl, L., & Ryan, J. (1996). *Schooling for change: Reinventing education for early adolescents.* Bristol, PA: Falmer. Evaluation of the policy and its impact can be found in Hargreaves, A., Earl, L., Moore, S., & Manning, S. (2001). *Learning to change.* San Francisco: Jossey Bass.

14. Barber, M. (2007). *Instruction to deliver: Fighting to transform Britain's public services.* London: Methuen, p. 32; Angus, D., & Mirel, J. (1999). *The failed promise of the American high school, 1890–1995.* New York: Teachers College Press.

15. Edley, C. (2002). *Keeping the promise of "No Child Left Behind": Success or failure depends largely on implementation by the U.S.* Cambridge, MA: Harvard Civil Rights Project; Taylor, W. (2006). Testimony of William L. Taylor Chairman, Citizens' Commission on civil rights before the commission on No Child Left Behind; National Council of La Raza (2007). *NCLB Works! New coalition launches breakthrough campaign.* Washington, DC: Author. Retrieved from http://www.nclr.org/content/news/detail/47399/

16. Fullan, M., Hill, P., & Crevola, C. (2006). *Breakthrough.* Thousand Oaks, CA: Corwin Press.

17. MacBeath, J., Gray, J., Cullen, J., Frost, D., Steward, S., & Swaffield, S. (2007). *Schools on the edge: Responding to challenging circumstances.* London: Paul Chapman; Fullan, M. (2005). *Leadership and sustainability: Systems thinkers in action.* London: Innovation Unit, Department for Education and Skills.

18. Oakes, J., & Lipton, M. (2002). Struggling educational equity and diverse communities: School reform as a social movement. *Journal of Educational Change, 3*(3–4), 383–406; Welner, K. (2001). *Legal rights, local wrongs: When community control collides with educational equity.* Albany, NY: State University of New York Press; Ball, S. (2003). *Class strategies and the education market: The middle classes and social advantage.* London: RoutledgeFalmer.

19. Ofsted Publications Centre (2004). *Reading for purpose and pleasure. An evaluation of the teaching of reading in primary schools.* London: Crown.

20. Nichols, S., & Berliner, D. (2007). *Collateral damage: How high-stakes testing corrupts America's schools.* Cambridge, MA: Harvard Education Press.

21. Jehlen, A. (2006). Moving beyond NCLB: There's plenty of room and opportunity for improvement. Retrieved from http://www.nea.org/home/13952 .htm; American Federation of Teachers. (2003). *Where we stand: Standard-based assessment and accountability.* Retrieved from http://www.aft.org/pubs-reports/ downloads/teachers/StandAssessRes.pdf

22. This evidence is drawn from a larger body of research reported in Hargreaves, A. (2003). *Teaching in the knowledge society: Education in the age of insecurity.* New York: Teachers College Press and Maidenhead, UK: Open University Press.

23. Cockburn, A., & Haydn, T. (2004). *Recruiting and retaining teachers: Understanding why teachers teach.* London: RoutledgeFalmer. For the recent data, see Milne, J. (July 11, 2008). NQTs quit in first few years of job. *Times Education Supplement.* Retrieved from http://www.tes.co.uk/article .aspx?storycode=2647089

24. Darling-Hammond, L. (2003). Keeping good teachers: Why it matters and what leaders can do. *Educational Leadership, 60*(8), 6–13.

25. See Hargreaves, *Teaching in the knowledge society.*

26. See Hargreaves & Fink, *Sustainable leadership.*

27. Koretz, D. (2008). *Measuring up: What educational testing really tells us.* Cambridge: Harvard University Press.

28. Nichols & Berliner, *Collateral damage.*

29. The New Progressive Declaration, signed July 10, 1996, by President Bill Clinton. Retrieved from http://www.ndol.org/ndol_ci.cfm?kaid=128&subid= 174&contentid=839

30. Blair & Schröder, *Europe: The Third Way*; Giddens, *The Third Way*; Giddens, *The Third Way and its critics*; Giddens, *The global Third Way debate.*

31. We are grateful to the incisive and insightful analysis of David Hartley on the impact of New Public management in education; see Hartley, D. (2007). The emergence of distributed leadership in education: Why now? *British Journal of Educational Studies, 55*(2), 202–214.

32. Hartley, The emergence of distributed leadership in education.

33. Alma Harris and one of us have been discovering this in the sport sector data in our current study of *Performing Beyond Expectations* (forthcoming) funded by the National College for School Leadership and the Specialist Schools and Academies Trust.

34. Barber, M. (2007). *Instruction to deliver: Fighting to transform Britain's public services*. London: Methuen.

35. Teachernet. (2003). School workforce remodelling. Retrieved from http://www.teachernet.gov.uk/wholeschool/remodelling/

36. Marley, D. (September 26, 2008). Teachers have designs on new buildings. Retrieved from http://www.tes.co.uk/article.aspx?storycode=6002962

37. These quotes are drawn from a wider set of responses reported in Hargreaves, *Teaching in the knowledge society*.

38. Fullan, *Leadership and sustainability*; Levin, B. (2008). *How to change 5000 schools: A practical and positive approach for leading change at every level*. Cambridge: Harvard Education Press.

39. Reported in Fullan, *Leadership and sustainability*. The most recent statement of Ontario policy at the time this book went to press was Government of Ontario (2008). *Reach every student: Energizing Ontario education*. Ontario: Queen's Printer for Ontario. Retrieved from http://www.edu.gov.on.ca/eng/document/energize/energize.pdf

40. National Center on Education and the Economy, *Tough choices or tough times*.

41. Cuban, L., & Usdan, M. (2003). *Powerful reforms with shallow roots: Improving America's urban schools*. New York: Teachers College Press.

42. Ewell, I. (2008). *BAEO-Gates Small Schools Project Report 2007–2008*. Retrieved from http://scoter.baeo.org/news_multi_media/(PCI-97)BAEO-Gates_Annual_Report_2008.PDF

43. Mitgang, L. D. (2008). *Becoming a leader: Preparing school principals for today's schools*. New York: The Wallace Foundation. Retrieved from http://www.wallacefoundation.org/SiteCollectionDocuments/WF/Knowledge%20Center/Attachments/PDF/Becoming%20a%20Leader.pdf

44. Explanations of the work of the New Schools Venture Fund can be found in Datnow, A., Park, V., & Wohlstetter, P. (2007). Achieving with data: How high performing schools use data to improve instruction for students. Retrieved from http://www.newschools.org/files/AchievingWithData.pdf; Datnow, A., Park, V., & Kennedy, B. (2008). Acting on data: How urban high schools use data to improve instruction. Retrieved from http://www.newschools.org/files/ActingonData.pdf

CHAPTER 2

1. Naisbitt, J. (1984). *Ten new directions transforming our lives*. New York: Warner Books.

2. Dewey, J. (1938). *Experience and education*. New York: Collier, p. 17.

3. Dewey, J. (1916). *Democracy and education*. New York: The MacMillan Company.

4. Fullan, M. (2006). *Turnaround leadership*. San Francisco: Jossey-Bass, p. 81.

5. New Commission on the Skills of the American Workforce. (2007). *Tough choices or tough times: The report of the new commission on the skills of the American workforce*. Washington, DC: National Center on Education and the Economy.

6. UNICEF (2007). *Child poverty in perspective: An overview of child well-being in rich countries, Innocenti Report Card 7*. Florence, Italy: UNICEF Innocenti Research Centre.

7. McKinsey & Company. (2007, September). *How the world's best-performing school systems come out on top*. Retrieved from www.mckinsey.com/clientservice/socialsector/resources/pdf/Worlds_School_systems_final.pdf

8. McKinsey & Company, *How the world's best-performing school systems come out on top*, p. 35.

9. McKinsey & Company, *How the world's best-performing school systems come out on top*, pp. 36–37.

10. Barber, M. (2007). *Instruction to deliver: Fighting to transform Britain's public services*. London: Methuen, pp. 79–101.

11. This National Challenge was launched by the secretary of state on June 10, 2008. In the Challenge, 30% of pupils in 638 identified schools were challenged to meet or to achieve 5*-C GCSEs, including English and math, by 2011. Retrieved from www.dcsf.gov.uk/nationalchallenge. For a critique, see Harris, A. (2009). Big change question: Does politics help or hinder educational change? *Journal of Educational Change, 10*(1), 63–67.

12. Barber, *Instruction to deliver*, pp. 64–65.

13. Barber, *Instruction to deliver*, p. 32.

14. Barber, *Instruction to deliver*, p. 348.

15. Barber, *Instruction to deliver*, p. 371.

16. Barber, *Instruction to deliver*.

17. Government of Ontario. (2008). *Reach every student: Energizing Ontario education*. Ontario: Queen's Printer for Ontario.

18. Langer, E. J. (1997). *The power of mindful learning*. Reading, MA: Addison-Wesley.

19. Argyris, C. (1976). *Increasing leadership effectiveness*. New York: Wiley; Argyris, C., & Schön, D. (1978). *Organizational learning: A theory of action perspective*. Reading, MA: Addison Wesley.

20. Sennett, R. (2008). *The craftsman*. New Haven, CT: Yale University Press, pp. 167–168.

21. Sennett, *The craftsman*, p. 171.

22. von Donnersmarck, F. H. (Writer/director). (2007). *The lives of others* [Motion picture]. United States: Sony Pictures Entertainment.

23. Rogers, J. (2006). Forces of accountability? The power of poor parents in NCLB. *Harvard Educational Review, 76*(4), 611–641.

24. Harris, A. (2006). Leading change in schools in difficulty. *Journal of Educational Change, 7*(1–2), 9–18.

25. Sanders, W. L., & Horn, S. P. (1994). The Tennessee value-added assessment system (TVAAS): Mixed-model methodology in educational assessment. *Journal of Personnel Evaluation in Education, 8*, 299–311; Sanders, W. L., & Horn, S. P. (1998). Research findings from the Tennessee value-added assessment system (TVAAS) database: Implications for educational evaluation and research. *Journal of Personnel Evaluation in Education, 12*(3), 247–256.

26. McCaffrey, D. S., Sass, T. R., & Lockwood, J. (2008). *The intertemporal stability of teacher effect estimates*. Nashville, TN: National Center on Performance Incentives, pp. 25, 40.

27. McCaffrey et al., *The intertemporal stability of teacher effect estimates*, p. 25.

28. Hargreaves, A., Shirley, D., Evans, M., Johnson, C., & Riseman, D. (2007). *The long and short of school improvement: Final evaluation of the raising achievement, transforming learning programme of the Specialist Schools and Academies Trust*. London: Specialist Schools and Academies Trust.

29. Gawande, A. (2002). *Complications: A surgeon's notes on an imperfect science*. New York: Metropolitan Books; Gawande, A. (2007). *Better: A surgeon's notes on performance*. New York: Picador.

30. Gawande, *Complications*, p. 7.

31. Gawande, *Better*.

32. Gawande, *Better*, p. 25.

33. Gawande, *Better*, p. 26.

34. Lewis, M. (2004). *Moneyball: The art of winning an unfair game*. New York: W. W. Norton & Company.

35. Lewis, *Moneyball*, p. xii.

36. Lewis, *Moneyball*, p. 15.

37. Lewis, *Moneyball*, p. 38.

38. This example is drawn from *Performing Beyond Expectations* (forthcoming), a study directed by Andy Hargreaves and Alma Harris, and funded

by the Specialist Schools and Academies Trust and the National College for School Leadership.

39. A. Hargreaves & Harris, *Performing Beyond Expectations.*

40. A. Hargreaves & Harris, *Performing Beyond Expectations.*

41. A. Hargreaves & Harris, *Performing Beyond Expectations.*

42. Datnow, A., Park, V., & Wohlstetter, P. (2007). *Achieving with data: How high performing schools use data to improve instruction for students.* Los Angeles, CA: Center on Educational Governance; Datnow, A., Park, V., & Kennedy, B. (2008). *Acting on data: How urban high schools use data to improve instruction.* Los Angeles, CA: Center on Educational Governance.

43. The term "turnstile world" is used by Sennett, R. (1998). *The corrosion of character: The personal consequences of work in the new capitalism.* New York: W. W. Norton & Company, p. 112.

44. Achinstein, B., & Ogawa, R. (2006, Spring). (In)fidelity: What the resistance of new teachers reveals about professional principles and prescriptive educational policies. *Harvard Educational Review, 76*(1), 30–63.

45. For more details on this study, see Hargreaves, A. (2003). *Teaching in the knowledge society: Education in the age of insecurity.* New York: Teachers College Press and Maidenhead, UK: Open University Press. For the magnet school in particular see Baker, M., & Foote, M. (2006). Changing spaces: Urban school interrelationships and the impact of standards-based reform. *Educational Administration Quarterly, 42*(1), 90–123.

46. This school has been studied as part of A. Hargreaves & Harris, *Performing Beyond Expectations* (forthcoming).

47. Shirley, D., & Hargreaves, A. (2006). Data-driven to distraction, *Education Week, 26*(6), 32–33.

48. For a discussion of schools as addictive organizations see Hargreaves, A., & Shirley, D. (2009). The persistence of presentism. *Teachers College Record, 111*(11). For the concept of addictive organizations read Schaef, A. W., & Fassel, D. (1988). *The addictive organization.* New York: Harper Collins.

49. A. Hargreaves et al., *The long and short of school improvement.*

50. Shirley, D. (2002). *Valley interfaith and school reform: Organizing for power in South Texas.* Austin, TX: University of Texas Press.

51. MacDonald, E., & Shirley, D. (2009). *The mindful teacher.* New York: Teachers College Press.

52. A. Hargreaves et al., *The long and short of school improvement.*

53. Durkheim, É. (1965). *Elementary forms of religious life.* New York: Free Press, p. 250.

54. Meštrović, S. G. (1997). *Postemotional society*. Thousand Oaks, CA: Sage Publications, p. 69.

55. Orwell, G. (1949). *1984*. New York: Harcourt, p. 32.

56. Christensen, C. M., Horn, M. B., Johnson, C. W. (2008). *Disrupting class: How disruptive innovation will change how the world works*. New York: McGraw-Hill; Christensen, C. M. (1997). *The innovator's dilemma: When new technologies cause great firms to fail*. Boston: Harvard Business School Press.

CHAPTER 3

1. Santayana, G. (1905). *The life of reason or the phases of human progress: Reason in common sense*. New York: Charles Scribner's Sons.

2. McLaughlin, M. (2008). Beyond "misery research"—New opportunities for implementation research, policy and practice. In C. Sugrue (Ed.) *The future of educational change: International perspectives* (pp. 175–190). New York: Routledge.

3. McKinsey & Company. (2007, September). *How the world's best-performing school systems come out on top*. Retrieved from www.mckinsey.com/clientservice/socialsector/resources/pdf/Worlds_School_systems_final.pdf

4. Gadamer, H.-G. (1991). *Truth and method*. New York: Crossroad, p. 302.

5. Stein, M., Hubbard, L., & Mehan, H. (2004). Reform ideas that travel far afield: The two cultures of reform in New York City's District #2 and San Diego. *Journal of Educational Change*, 5(2), 161–197.

6. This report on Finland draws on an evaluation report of leadership and school improvement in Finland coauthored by one of us for OECD. See Hargreaves, A., Halász, G., & Pont, B. (2008). The Finnish approach to system leadership. In Pont, B. Nusche. D. & Hopkins, D. (Eds.). (2008). *Improving school leadership, Vol. 2: Case studies on system leadership*. Paris: OECD. Other key resources on educational performance and reform strategies in Finland include Aho, E., Pitkänen, K., & Sahlberg, P. (2006). *Policy development and reform principles of basic and secondary education in Finland since 1968*. Washington, DC: World Bank; Castells, M., & Himanen, P. (2004). *The information society and the welfare state: The Finnish model*. New York: Oxford University Press; Grubb, W. N. (2007, October). Dynamic inequality and intervention: Lessons from a small country. *Phi Delta Kappan*, 105–114; Sahlberg, P. (2006). Education reform for raising economic competitiveness. *Journal of Educational Change*, 7(4), 259–287.

7. UNICEF (2007). *Child poverty in perspective: An overview of child well-being in rich countries, Innocenti Report Card 7*. Florence, Italy: UNICEF

Innocenti Research Centre. Retrieved from http://www.unicef-irc.org/publications/pdf/rc7_eng.pdf

8. See Sheffi, Y. (2005) *The resilient enterprise: Overcoming vulnerability for competititve advantage.* Cambridge: MIT Press, pp. 7–8. For more information on Nokia, see Haikio, M. (2002). *Nokia, the inside story.* London: Prentice Hall.

9. This section draws on our original evaluation of *RATL*, reported in Hargreaves, A., Shirley, D., Evans, M., Johnson, C., & Riseman, D. (2007). *The long and short of school improvement: Final evaluation of the Raising Achievement, Transforming Learning programme of the Specialist Schools and Academies Trust.* London: Specialist Schools and Academies Trust.

10. A. Hargreaves et al., *The long and short of school improvement,* p. 36.

11. For an evaluation that reports favorably on the success of *RATL* in its subsequent phase of transformation in a sample of 20 schools, see Harris, A., Allen, T., & Goodall, J. (2008). *Capturing transformation: How schools secure and sustain improvement.* London: Specialist Schools and Academies Trust.

12. A. Hargreaves first applied the term "market fundamentalism" to education (Hargreaves, A. [2003]. *Teaching in the knowledge society: Education in the age of insecurity.* New York: Teachers College Press, p. 4). Its original use can be found in Soros, G. (2002). *George Soros on globalization.* New York: Perseus.

13. Warren, M. R. (2001). *Dry bones rattling: Community building to revitalize American democracy.* Princeton, NJ: Princeton University Press; Oakes, J., & Rogers, J. (2006). *Learning power: Organizing for education and justice.* New York: Teachers College Press; Payne, C. (2007). *I've got the light of freedom: The organizing tradition and the Mississippi freedom struggle.* Berkeley, CA: University of California Press.

14. Obama, B. (1995). *Dreams from my father: A story of race and inheritance.* New York: Times Books.

15. Stone, C., Henig, J., Jones, B., & Pierannunzi, C. (2001). *Building civic capacity: The politics of reforming urban schools.* Lawrence, KS: University Press of Kansas.

16. Skocpol, T. (2004). *Diminished democracy: From membership to management in American civic life.* Norman, OK: University of Oklahoma Press.

17. Stone et al., *Building civic capacity,* pp. 85–86.

18. Usdan, M. D., & Cuban, L. (2003). *Powerful reforms with shallow roots: Improving America's urban schools.* New York: Teachers College Press.

19. Academy for Educational Development. (2006). *Lead teacher report: Second year report submitted to the community collaborative to improve Bronx schools.* Washington, DC: Author.

20. Shah, S., & Mediratta, K. (2008, April). Negotiating reform: Young people's leadership in the educational arena. *New Directions in Youth Development*, pp. 43–59.

21. Warren, M. R. (2005). Communities and schools: A new view of urban education reform. *Harvard Educational Review, 75*, 133–173; Warren, M. R., Hong, S., Rubin, C. H., & Uy, P. S. (2009). Beyond the bake sale: A community-based relational approach to parent engagement in schools. *Teachers College Record, 111*(9). Retrieved from http://www.tcrecord.org, ID Number: 15390.

22. Shirley, D. (1997). *Community organizing for urban school reform.* Austin, TX: University of Texas Press.

23. Oakes & Rogers, *Learning power.*

24. Obama, *Dreams from my father.*

25. Mediratta, K., Shah, S., & McAlister, S. (2008). *Organized communities, stronger schools: A preview of research findings.* Providence, RI: Annenberg Institute for School Reform.

26. Bryk, A. S., & Schneider, B. (2005). *Trust in schools: A core resource for improvement.* New York: Russell Sage Foundation. On the importance of trust and betrayal in education, see also Hargreaves, A. (2002). Teaching and betrayal. *Teachers and Teaching: Theory and Practice, 8*(3/4), 393–407

27. This school district case study is drawn from data collected in the *Performing Beyond Expectations* study conducted by Andy Hargreaves and Alama Harris (forthcoming) in collaboration with team member Alan Boyle, and funded by the Specialist Schools and Academies Trust and the National College for School Leadership.

28. The first classic community study of this "East End" working-class community was Young, M., & Willmott, P. (1957). *Family and kinship in East London.* London: Routledge & Kegan Paul. (Reprinted 1992 and 2007.) Additional information on Tower Hamlets is available in a special themed issue of the Annenberg Institute for School Reform's (2008) *Voices in Urban Education, 21.*

29. Fletcher, C., Caron, M., & Williams, W. (1985). *Schools on trial.* Milton Keynes, UK: Open University Press; Watts. J. (Ed.). (1977). *The Countesthorpe experience.* London: George Allen & Unwin.

30. Hargreaves & Harris (forthcoming). These benign effects of workforce remodeling on relationships between teachers and communities in disadvantaged schools have also been documented by Gordon, J. A. (2008). Community responsive schools, mixed housing and community regeneration. *Journal of Education Policy, 23*(2), 181–192.

31. Finn, J. D., & Achilles, C. M. (1999). Tennessee's class size study: Findings, implications, misconceptions. *Educational Evaluation and Policy Analysis, 21*(2), 97–109; Nye, B., Hedges, L. V., & Konstantopoulos, S. (2000).

The effects of small classes on academic achievement: The results of the Tennessee class size experiment. *American Educational Research Journal, 37*(1), 123–151; Word, E. R., Johnston, J., Bain, H. P., & Fulton, B. D. (1990). *The State of Tennessee's Student/Teacher Achievement Ratio (STAR) Project: Technical Report 1985–90.* Nashville, TN: Tennessee State University.

32. Shirley, D. (2006). Street-level democrats: Realizing the potential of school, university, and community coalitions. *The Educational Forum, 70*(2), 116–122.

33. Barber, M. (2007). *Instruction to deliver: Fighting to transform Britain's public services.* London: Methuen, p. 70.

CHAPTER 4

1. Darling-Hammond, L. (2008). Teaching and the change wars: The professionalism hypothesis. In A. Hargreaves & M. Fullan (Eds.), *Change wars* (pp. 45–68). Bloomington, IN: Solution Tree.

2. Haidt, J. (2006). *The happiness hypothesis: Finding modern truth in ancient wisdom.* New York: Basic Books; Hargreaves, A. (2001). The emotional geographies of teaching. *Teachers College Record, 103*(6), 1056–1080; Hargreaves, A. (2001). The emotional geographies of teachers' relations with their colleagues. *International Journal of Educational Research, 35,* 503–527; Seligman, M.E.P. (2002). *Authentic happiness: Using the new positive psychology to realize your potential for lasting fulfillment.* New York: Free Press.

3. Werner, E., & Smith, R. (1992). *Overcoming the odds: High risk children from birth to adulthood.* Ithaca, NY: Cornell University Press; Werner, E., & Smith, R. (2001). *Journeys from childhood to the midlife: Risk, resilience, and recovery.* New York: Cornell University Press.

4. Werner & Smith, *Overcoming the odds*; Werner & Smith, *Journeys from childhood to the midlife.*

5. Harris, A. (2006). Leading change in schools in difficulty. *Journal of Educational Change, 17*(1–2), 9–18.

6. Tucker, M. S. (2009). Industrial benchmarking: A research method for education. In A. Hargreaves & Fullan, *Change wars*, pp. 117–133.

7. For example, on the eve of the G-20 summit in November 2008, President George W. Bush offered a vigorous defense of laissez-faire capitalism. For the text of the speech, see "President Bush Discusses Financial Markets and World Economy." Retrieved from http://www.heartland.org/article/24166/President_Bush_Discusses_Financial_Markets_and_World_Economy_.html

8. See UNICEF. (2007). *Child poverty in perspective: An overview of child well-being in rich countries, Innocenti Report Card 7.* Florence, Italy: UNICEF Innocenti Research Centre.

9. This is now advocated in many places, but especially in Fullan, M. (2008). *The six secrets of change: What the best leaders do to help their organizations survive and thrive.* San Francisco: Jossey-Bass.

10. See, for example, Barber, M. (2008). From system effectiveness to system improvement: Reform paradigms and relationships. In A. Hargreaves & Fullan, *Change wars*, pp. 87–88.

11. This is as advocated in the classic United Nations Educational, Scientific, and Cultural Organization (UNESCO) report by Delors, J. (1996). *Learning: the treasure within—Report to UNESCO of the International Commission on Education for the twenty-first century.* Paris: Author; see also Sahlberg, P. (2006). Education reform for raising economic competitiveness. *Journal of Educational Change, 7*(4), 259–287.

12. Weil, S. (1997). *The need for roots: Prelude to a declaration of duties towards mankind.* New York: Routledge.

13. Obama, B. (1995). *Dreams from my father: A story of race and inheritance.* New York: Times Books.

14. As reported in Fullan, M. (2006). *Turnaround leadership.* San Francisco: Jossey-Bass; Fullan, *The six secrets of change.*

15. See, for example, Harris, A., Bennett, N., & Reynolds, D. (Eds.). (2005). *School effectiveness and school improvement: Alternative perspectives.* London: Continuum International; Reynolds, D. (Ed.). (1985). *Studying school effectiveness.* London: Falmer Press.

16. Carter, S. C. (1999). *No excuses: Seven principals of low-income schools who set the standard for high achievement.* Washington, DC: The Heritage Foundation; Carter, S.C. (2000). *No excuses: Lessons from 21 high-performing, high-poverty schools.* Washington, DC: The Heritage Foundation.

17. Harris et al., *School effectiveness and school improvement.*

18. Fleisch, B. (2008). *Primary education in crisis: Why South African schoolchildren underachieve in reading and mathematics.* Cape Town, South Africa: Juta.

19. Berliner, D. (2006). Our impoverished view of educational research. *Teachers College Record, 108*(6), 949–995. In particular, see tables on pp. 964–966.

20. Berliner, *Our impoverished view of educational research.*

21. Townsend, T. (2008, September). *Third millennium leaders: Thinking and acting both locally and globally.* Keynote speech presented at Commonwealth Council for Educational Administration and Management (CCEAM) Conference, Durban, South Africa.

22. Information on Building Schools for the Future (BSF). Retrieved from http://www.teachernet.gov.uk/management/resourcesfinanceandbuilding/bsf/

23. S. Alinsky, cited in Shirley, D. (1997). *Community organizing for urban school reform*. Austin, TX: University of Texas Press, pp. 244–245.

24. Honoré, C. (2008) *Under pressure: rescuing our children from the culture of hyper-parenting*. New York: HarperOne.

25. Apple, M. (2001). *Educating the "right" way: Markets, standards, God, and inequality*. New York: RoutledgeFalmer.

26. These cases are drawn from Hargreaves, A., & Shaw, P. (2006). *Knowledge and skills development in developing and transitional economies*. An analysis of World Bank/DfID knowledge and skills for the modern economy. Report to the World Bank. Chestnut Hill, MA: Boston College.

27. A. Hargreaves & Shaw, *Knowledge and skills development*.

28. Obama, *Dreams from my father*.

29. On student involvement in change, see Rudduck, J., Day, J., & Wallace, G. (1997). Students' perspectives on school improvement. In A. Hargreaves (Ed.), *Rethinking educational change with heart and mind* (the 1997 *ASCD Yearbook*, pp. 73–91), Alexandria, VA: Association for Supervision and Curriculum Development; Ben Levin, "Sustainable, large-scale education renewal," *Journal of Educational Change, 8*(4), 323–336.

30. Grubb, Dynamic inequality and intervention; Honoré, C. (2004). *In praise of slowness: How a worldwide movement is challenging the cult of speed*. New York: HarperCollins.

31. Mediratta, K., Shah, S., & McAlister, S. (2008). *Organized communities, stronger schools: A preview of research findings*. Providence, RI: Annenberg Institute for School Reform; McLaughlin, M., Scott, W. R., Deschenes, S., Hopkins, K., & Newman, A. (2009). *Between movement and establishment: Organizations advocating for youth*. Palo Alto, CA: Stanford University Press; Oakes, J., & Rogers, J. (2006). *Learning power: Organizing for education and justice*. New York: Teachers College Press; Su, C. (2009). *Streetwise for book smarts: Grassroots organizing and education reform in the Bronx*. Ithaca, NY: Cornell University Press.

32. Department for Children, Schools and Families (2008). *Personalised learning: A practical guide*. London: DCSF Publications. Retrieved from http://publications.teachernet.gov.uk/eOrderingDownload/00844-2008DOM-EN.pdf; Miliband, D. (2004). *Personalised learning: Building a new relationship with schools*. London: DCSF Publications. Retrieved from http://publications.teachernet.gov.uk/eOrderingDownload/personalised-learning.pdf

33. Hargreaves, D. (2006). *A new shape for schooling?* London: Specialist Schools and Academies Trust, p. 24.

34. D. Hargreaves, *A new shape for schooling?* On the importance of projects versus ubiquitous short lessons within the concept of personalization, see

Hargreaves, D. (2004). *Learning for life: The foundations for lifelong learning.* London: Policy Press, p. 2.

35. European Commission. (2001). *A memorandum on lifelong learning.* Brussels: European Commission; Organisation for Economic Co-operation and Development (OECD). (1996). *Lifelong learning for all.* Paris: Author.

36. D. Hargreaves, *A new shape for schooling?*, p. 3.

37. D. Hargreaves, *A new shape for schooling?*, p. 2. In late 2008, D. Hargreaves testified to the House of Commons Children's Committee that he favored the analogy with business, which had geared itself to meet a customized market. At the same time, he contended, given increasing contentiousness in the use of the term, he only now used the term if pressed and felt that it was a "total waste of time trying to find a definition." See Baker, M. (2008). "Let's not get personal." Retrieved from http://news.bbc.co.uk/2/hi/uk_news/education/7741943.stm

38. Wagner, T. (2008). *The global achievement gap.* New York: Basic.

39. Bauman, Z. (2008). *The art of life.* Cambridge, UK: Polity.

40. MacDonald, E., & Shirley, D. (2006). Growing teacher leadership in the urban context: The power of partnerships. In K. R. Howey, L. M. Post, & N. L. Zimpher (Eds.), *Recruiting, preparing and retaining teachers for urban schools* (pp. 125–144). *Washington,* DC: American Association of Colleges of Teacher Education; MacDonald, E., & Shirley, D. (2009). *The mindful teacher.* New York: Teachers College Press.

41. Ancess, J. (2003). *Beating the odds: High schools as communities of commitment.* New York: Teachers College Press; Perry, T., Steele, C., & Hillard, A. (2003). *Young, gifted, and black: Promoting high achievement among African-American students.* Boston: Beacon Press; Scheurich, J. (1998). Cultural characteristics populated mainly by low-SES children of color: Core beliefs and highly successful and loving, public elementary schools. *Urban Education, 33*(4), 451–491.

42. Hess, F. (2001). *Tear down this wall: The case for a radical overhaul of teacher certification.* Washington, DC: Progressive Policy Institute.

43. This percentage is an estimate based on data for the number of teachers certified by the NBPTS (as reported by NBPTS, retrieved from http://www.nbpts.org/resources/nbct_directory/nbcts_by_year), compared with the total number of public elementary and secondary teachers in 2005 (as reported in U.S. Census Bureau, Statistical Abstract of the United States, 2008. Education: elementary and secondary education: Staff and finances. Washington, DC, 2007. Retrieved from http://www.census.gov/compendia/statab/cats/education/elementary_and_secondary_education_staff_and_finances.html).

44. For an extended discussion on this issue, see Hargreaves, A., & Evans, R. (1997). *Beyond educational reform.* Buckingham, UK: Open University Press.

45. For information on TURN, see www.turnexchange.net

46. Lortie, D. C. (1975). *Schoolteacher: A sociological study.* Chicago: University of Chicago Press.

47. Hargreaves, A. (2003). *Teaching in the knowledge society.* New York: Teachers College Press.

48. A. Hargreaves, *Teaching in the knowledge society.*

49. The term "contrived collegiality" is introduced and discussed in Hargreaves, A. (1994). *Changing teachers, changing times: Teachers' work and culture in the postmodern age.* New York: Teachers' College Press.

50. See Hargreaves, A. (2007). Leading professional learning communities. In A. M. Blankstein, P. D. Houston, R. W. Cole (Eds.). (2008). *Sustaining professional learning communities.* Thousand Oaks, CA: Corwin Press.

51. MacDonald & Shirley, *The mindful teacher.*

52. Sennett, R. (2008). *The craftsman.* New Haven, CT: Yale University Press.

53. Alinsky, S. (1965). The war on poverty—political pornography. *Journal of Social Issues, 11*(1), 41–47. Quote is on p. 42.

54. This percentage was calculated after reviewing the third edition of Florida's Educational Leadership Examination (FELE) competencies and skills. Retrieved on November 25, 2008, from http://www.fldoe.org/asp/fele/. The State Board of Education approved these FELE changes in June 2008, and the Florida Department of Education began administration of the new examination in January 2009.

55. On the reasons for principal supply shortage related to the conditions of educational change and work overload, see, for example, PriceWaterhouse Coopers. (2007). *Independent study into school leadership.* Nottingham, UK: Department for Education and Skills; Hewitt, P., Pijanowski, J., Carnine, L., & Denny, G. (2008). *The status of school leadership in Arkansas.* Fayetteville: University of Arkansas; Cusick, P. A. (2002). *A study of Michigan's school principal shortage.* East Lansing, MI: Education Policy Center, Michigan State University.

56. Hatch, T. (2002). When improvement plans collide. *Phi Delta Kappan, 83*(8), 626–634.

57. For more information on distributed leadership, see Spillane, J. P. (2006). *Distributed leadership.* San Francisco: Jossey-Bass; Fink, D., & Hargreaves, A. (2008). Distributed leadership: Delivery or democracy. *Journal of Educational Administration, 46*(2), 229–240.

58. The concept of "sustainable leadership" and the seven principles drawn from it were first discussed in Hargreaves, A., & Fink, D. (2006). *Sustainable leadership.* San Francisco: Jossey-Bass.

59. See, for example, Hill, R., & Matthews, P. (2008, November 21). Captains to steer through the storm. *Times Educational Supplement,* pp. 30–31;

Hill, R., & Matthews, P. (2008). *Schools leading schools: The power and potential of national leaders of education*. Nottingham, UK: National College for School Leadership.

60. On the necessity of balancing emergence and design, see Capra, F. (2002). *The hidden connection: A science for sustainable living*. New York: Harper Collins. On the application of Capra's ideas to sustainable improvement and leadership, see Fink & Hargreaves, Distributed leadership.

61. Hargreaves, D. (2004). *Education epidemic: Transforming secondary schools through innovation networks*. London: Demos.

62. Castells, M. (2001). *The Internet galaxy*. Oxford: Oxford University Press.

63. Ainscow M., Dyson A., Goldrick, S., Kerr, K., & Miles, S. (2008). *Equity in education: Responding to context*. Manchester, UK: Center for Equity in Education, University of Manchester.

64. Lindsay, G., Muijs, D., Chapman, C., & Harris, A. (2007). *Final report of the federations policy*. London: Department for Education and Skills.

65. Nichols, S., & Berliner, D. (2007). *Collateral damage: How high-stakes testing corrupts America's schools*. Cambridge: Harvard Education Press; Booher-Jennings, J. (2005). Below the bubble: Educational triage and the Texas accountability system. *American Educational Research Journal, 42*(2), 231–268; McNeill, L. M. (2000). *Contradictions of school reform: The educational costs of standardized testing*. New York: Routledge; A. Hargreaves, *Teaching in the knowledge society*.

66. Rust, K. F., Krenzke, T., Qian, J., & Johnson, E. G. (2001) Sample design for the national assessment. In Allen, N. L., Donoghue, J. R., & Schoeps, T. L. (Eds.) (2001). *The NAEP 1998 technical report*. Washington, DC: National Center for Education Statistics, pp. 31–50.

67. Hargreaves, D. H. (2004). *Learning for life: The foundations for lifelong learning*. Bristol, UK: Policy Press.

68. Skerrett, A. (2008). Going the race way: Biographical influences on multicultural and antiracist English curriculum practices. *Teaching & Teacher Education, 24*(7), 1813–1826; Skerrett, A., & Hargreaves, A. (2008). Student diversity and secondary school change in a context of increasingly standardized reform. *American Educational Research Journal, 45*(4), 913–945.

69. Nathan, L. (2008). What's been lost in the bubbles. *Educational Leadership, 66*(2), 52–55.

70. This example is drawn from the *Performing Beyond Expectations* study (forthcoming) directed by Andy Hargreaves and Alma Harris.

71. Frost, R. (1946). *The poems of Robert Frost*. New York: Random House, 177.

INDEX

∷

CORWIN
A SAGE Company

The Corwin logo—a raven striding across an open book—represents the union of courage and learning. Corwin is committed to improving education for all learners by publishing books and other professional development resources for those serving the field of PreK–12 education. By providing practical, hands-on materials, Corwin continues to carry out the promise of its motto: **"Helping Educators Do Their Work Better."**

The Ontario Principals' Council (OPC) is a voluntary professional association for principals and vice-principals in Ontario's public school system.We believe that exemplary leadership results in outstanding schools and improved student achievement. To this end, we foster quality leadership through world-class professional services and supports. As an ISO 9001 registered organization, we are committed to our statement that "quality leadership is our principal product."

NSDC's purpose: Every educator engages in effective professional learning every day so every student achieves.